Unveiling the Magic of Christmas Baking

A Whisk of Holiday Magic: Introduction to Christmas Baking

Emma Stewart

Table of Contents

INTRODUCTION

Welcome to "Unveiling the Magic of Christmas Baking: A Whisk of Holiday Magic," a delightful journey into the heart of festive culinary traditions. As the holiday season unfolds its magical embrace, there's no better way to immerse yourself in the joyous spirit than through the art of Christmas baking. This e-book is your companion in unlocking the secrets, stories, and enchantments surrounding the world of Christmas treats.

The season of merriment is inseparable from the sweet symphony of baking, and in these pages, we invite you to explore the rich tapestry of Christmas baking traditions. From the humble beginnings of ancient rituals to the modern-day twists on classic recipes, our journey will unfold the layers of history, culture, and creativity that make Christmas baking a cherished global phenomenon.

In these chapters, we will guide you through the essential tools, ingredients, and techniques that define the magical realm of Christmas baking. From classic sugar cookies and gingerbread masterpieces to decadent yule log cakes and festive bread, each chapter unveils the secrets behind beloved treats that have stood the test of time. You'll discover the joy of crafting edible gifts, learn the art of chocolate making, and find inspiration in creating a magical Christmas atmosphere in your kitchen.

But this e-book is more than just a collection of recipes; it's an invitation to create lasting memories with family and friends. As you embark on this journey, you'll find troubleshooting tips, reflections on global Christmas baking traditions, and guidance on starting your family baking rituals.

So, preheat your oven, dust off your rolling pin, and get ready to infuse your home with the irresistible aroma of holiday cheer. "Unveiling the Magic of Christmas Baking" is not just a guide; it's a celebration of the warmth, love, and magic that come alive in every kitchen during this most beautiful time of the year. Let the whisk of holiday magic whisk you into the enchanting world of Christmas baking.

CHAPTER I

The History of Christmas Baking

Origins of Christmas Baking Traditions

The origins of Christmas baking traditions can be traced back to ancient times when the roots of these festive practices were deeply intertwined with cultural, religious, and historical developments. One of the earliest influences on Christmas baking can be found in ancient Rome, where the festival of Saturnalia, held in mid-December, involved preparing and sharing special foods. Romans exchanged offerings of homemade sweets, a tradition that laid the foundation for exchanging holiday treats during the Christmas season.

As Christianity began to spread and assimilate various customs, the celebration of Christmas evolved. The Middle Ages witnessed the emergence of rich, spiced breads known as "infanti," a precursor to modern-day fruitcakes. These sweet and savory breads, filled with nuts, fruits, and spices, became famous for their taste and symbolic significance. The use of exotic spices, often a luxury in medieval times, reflected the desire to create unique, opulent treats reserved for celebratory occasions.

With the passing of centuries, Christmas baking traditions continued to evolve and diversify across different regions. In Germany, the concept of the Christmas tree was introduced in the 16th century, and with it came the tradition of decorating the tree with edible ornaments. Nuts, fruits, and baked goods adorned the branches, emphasizing the communal and festive nature of the season. Meanwhile, the Yule log cake, or "julekake," symbolized the winter solstice celebrations in Scandinavia. Families would bake and share this sweet, spiced bread to mark the return of longer days and the triumph of light over darkness.

The influence of Queen Victoria and Prince Albert further popularized certain Christmas traditions in the 19th century. The royal couple, who embraced the Christmas tree tradition from Prince Albert's German heritage, were depicted in an influential illustration featuring the royal family gathered around a lavishly decorated Christmas tree. This imagery, widely circulated in newspapers, solidified the association of Christmas with festive decorations, including edible treats.

In the United States, the 19th century saw the fusion of diverse cultural influences, shaping the Christmas baking landscape. German immigrants introduced the concept of the Christmas cookie, a tradition that quickly gained popularity. The iconic gingerbread cookie, often shaped into festive figures, became a staple of American Christmas celebrations. Meanwhile, the American adaptation of the English fruitcake evolved into a cherished holiday dessert, symbolizing abundance and goodwill.

The 20th century witnessed the commercialization of Christmas, with the emergence of mass-produced holiday treats and the popularization of certain iconic sweets. Despite its mixed reputation, the classic fruitcake maintained its status as a traditional Christmas delicacy. The advent of modern appliances and innovations in the food industry further democratized the baking process, allowing families to engage in holiday baking with greater ease.

In recent decades, interest in artisanal and personalized Christmas baking has been revived. The do-it-yourself movement and the rise of food blogs and social media have encouraged individuals to explore unique recipes, experiment with flavors, and share their creations with a global audience. Traditional recipes are passed down through generations, while new and inventive ideas continuously enrich the tapestry of Christmas baking traditions.

In conclusion, the origins of Christmas baking traditions are deeply rooted in a diverse tapestry of historical, cultural, and religious influences. From the ancient Roman festival of Saturnalia to the medieval spiced bread, the German Christmas tree tradition, to the American adaptation of Christmas cookies, each era and culture has contributed to the rich mosaic of festive treats enjoyed during the holiday season. The evolution of Christmas baking reflects changes in culinary preferences and the enduring human desire to create, share, and savor special moments during this season of joy and togetherness.

Evolution of Holiday Treats Across Cultures

The evolution of holiday treats across cultures is a fascinating journey that traverses centuries, bridging diverse traditions and culinary landscapes. Each culture's festive table reflects its unique history, religious practices, and local ingredients, creating a rich tapestry of flavors and customs that transcend borders and periods.

In ancient civilizations, observance of religious festivals often involved preparing and consuming special foods. In Mesopotamia, the celebration of the New Year, known as Akitu, featured sweetened barley cakes, symbolizing renewal and abundance. Similarly, the Egyptians honored the gods with honey and baked goods offerings during their religious festivals, emphasizing the sacred connection between food and spiritual rituals.

The advent of Christianity brought about the integration of religious observances into the culinary traditions of various cultures. In medieval Europe, the celebration of Christmas was marked by the preparation of spiced breads and fruit-filled pastries, often shaped into elaborate designs to symbolize the Nativity story. These early versions of Christmas treats, including the famous Yule log cake, laid the foundation for the festive confections that would become integral to holiday celebrations across the continent.

As Europe entered the Renaissance, global exploration and trade introduced many new ingredients to the culinary landscape. Once considered rare and precious, spices such as cinnamon, nutmeg, and cloves became more widely available. This influx of exotic flavors enriched holiday treats, creating a fusion of indigenous and foreign ingredients that contributed to the development of distinctive regional delicacies.

In Germany, the concept of the Christmas tree, along with its edible decorations, gained popularity in the 16th century. Nuts, fruits, and baked goods adorned the tree, symbolizing abundance and prosperity. The tradition of gingerbread cookies shaped into festive figures, known as Lebkuchen, became an integral part of German Christmas celebrations. These intricately decorated cookies delighted the taste buds and served as edible works of art.

In the United Kingdom, the Victorian era witnessed the popularization of Christmas cards and imagery that celebrated the festive season. Illustrations depicting families gathered around lavishly decorated tables laden with holiday treats became iconic, shaping the visual representation of Christmas. The Christmas pudding, a decadent and steamed dessert filled with dried fruits and spices, became a cherished centerpiece of the British holiday feast.

In Scandinavia, the celebration of Saint Lucia's Day became synonymous with the tradition of baking saffron-infused sweet bread and buns. The aromatic and golden-hued treats, such as Lussekatter, are enjoyed in honor of Saint Lucia, the bearer of light during the dark winter months. This tradition showcases the deep connection between cultural celebrations, religious observances, and the art of baking.

Across the Atlantic, the fusion of diverse cultural influences in the United States gave rise to a unique blend of holiday treats. German immigrants introduced the concept of the Christmas cookie, a tradition that quickly gained popularity. Gingerbread houses became a holiday activity, marrying culinary creativity with architectural flair. The American adaptation of the English fruitcake evolved into a symbol of abundance and goodwill, often passed down through generations.

In Mexico, the celebration of Las Posadas involves sharing traditional treats such as buñuelos, crispy fried dough drizzled with syrup, or sprinkled with cinnamon and sugar. Tamales, a labor-intensive but beloved holiday dish, showcases the artistry of masa (corn dough) combined with various fillings. These treats, deeply rooted in Mexican culture, reflect the joyous and communal spirit of the season.

In the Middle East, the celebration of Eid al-Fitr, marking the end of Ramadan, is accompanied by various sweets and desserts. Dates, a symbol of the holy month, are often incorporated into recipes, such as ma'amoul, delicate shortbread-like cookies filled with dates, nuts, or figs. These treats' intricate patterns and shapes reflect the craftsmanship associated with festive baking in the region.

In East Asia, the Lunar New Year is celebrated with many sweet delicacies that symbolize prosperity and good fortune. In China, nian gao, a sticky rice cake, is a traditional New Year treat that brings good luck and prosperity. Meanwhile, in Japan, the celebration of shiatsu involves the preparation of osechi ryori, a collection of beautifully arranged and symbolic dishes, including sweet treats like mochi and wagashi.

As the world has become more interconnected, globalization has led to the exchange of culinary traditions and the fusion of diverse influences. The holiday treats enjoyed today often reflect a global palate, incorporating flavors and ingredients from different corners of the world. International cuisines influence one another, creating a mosaic of culinary diversity that transcends cultural boundaries.

In conclusion, the evolution of holiday treats across cultures is a testament to the enduring connection between food, celebration, and cultural identity. From ancient religious rituals to modern-day festivities, baking has played a central role in shaping the traditions and flavors associated with holidays worldwide. Whether it's the spiced breads of medieval Europe, the intricate gingerbread creations of Germany, or the symbolic treats enjoyed during the Lunar New Year, each culture contributes its unique chapter to the global story of festive baking, creating a delicious legacy that continues to evolve and inspire.

CHAPTER II

Essential Tools and Ingredients

Must-Have Kitchen Gadgets for Christmas Baking

The art of Christmas baking is a festive tradition that brings joy, warmth, and the irresistible aroma of sweet treats into our homes. Having the right kitchen gadgets is essential to embark on this culinary journey with efficiency and creativity. As we delve into the world of Christmas baking, several must-have tools emerge as invaluable companions in the quest to create delectable and visually stunning holiday treats.

A fundamental tool in any baker's arsenal is a reliable stand mixer. Whether it's the iconic KitchenAid or another trusted brand, a stand mixer simplifies the process of mixing, beating, and kneading, allowing for consistent and thoroughly blended ingredients. The versatile attachments, from the whisk for whipping cream to the dough hook for kneading bread, make a stand mixer an indispensable workhorse in the Christmas baking kitchen.

Accurate measurements are crucial in baking, and high-quality measuring cups and spoons ensure precision in ingredient quantities. Whether measuring flour for cookies or spices for gingerbread, these tools provide the accuracy needed to achieve the perfect balance of flavors and textures in festive treats.

In the realm of precision, a digital kitchen scale takes accuracy to the next level. Especially when dealing with ingredients like flour, where the density can vary, a scale ensures that measurements are spot-on, resulting in consistent and reliable baking outcomes. This is particularly important when tackling intricate recipes or experimenting with new flavor combinations.

Rolling out dough for cookies, pies, or pastries is a common task in Christmas baking, and a reliable rolling pin is necessary. Opting for a rolling pin with adjustable thickness settings provides versatility for various recipes. Additionally, a non-stick surface ensures smooth and even rolling, making the process more efficient and enjoyable.

Cookie cutters are indispensable for the precise and decorative cutting of cookie shapes or intricate designs in the rolled dough. From classic holiday shapes like stars and snowflakes to whimsical designs that capture the festive spirit, a diverse collection of cookie cutters allows for creative expression in every batch of Christmas cookies.

A good-quality set of mixing bowls in various sizes is an essential foundation for any baking endeavor. Whether preparing wet or dry ingredients, having multiple bowls facilitates an organized and efficient workflow. Stainless steel or glass bowls are ideal for durability and ease of cleaning.

When it comes to baking cookies, achieving uniform sizes ensures even baking. A cookie scoop, available in various sizes, allows for consistent portions of dough, resulting in perfectly shaped and evenly baked cookies. This not only enhances the visual appeal of the treats but also contributes to a uniform texture.

The precision of decorating plays a pivotal role in the visual allure of Christmas treats. Piping bags and tips are indispensable for creating intricate designs, frosting cookies, or embellishing cakes. Various tips allow for versatility in decorating techniques, from intricate details to bold swirls of frosting.

A rotating cake turntable is a game-changer in the world of Christmas baking, where delicate decorations and intricate designs are prevalent. This tool allows for smooth and controlled icing and decorating, ensuring that every angle of the baked creation receives the attention it deserves. The rotating feature eliminates the need to constantly adjust the position of the baked goods, providing a seamless decorating experience.

For those who enjoy the artistry of icing and decorating,

a set of offset spatulas becomes an extension of the hand. These tools enable the precise spreading of frosting, smooth surfaces, and intricate detailing. The offset design provides optimal control and maneuverability, allowing for professional-looking finishes on cakes and cookies.

Investing in a quality baking sheet is paramount to

achieve perfectly flaky pie crusts or evenly baked cookies. Opting for sheets with a non-stick surface or parchment paper ensures easy release and minimal mess. Additionally, rimmed sheets prevent potential spills or drips, making them versatile for baking tasks.

In the realm of festive desserts, the allure of beautifully

shaped cakes is undeniable. With their intricate designs, Bundt pans transform simple cake recipes into stunning centerpieces. The non-stick coating ensures easy release, preserving the details of the pan's design and simplifying the process of creating visually striking cakes.

A kitchen thermometer is a tool that often goes

overlooked but is crucial for achieving precise results in baking. From checking the internal temperature of bread for doneness to ensuring that custards and candies reach the correct temperature, a reliable thermometer is a baker's best friend, providing accuracy and consistency in every creation.

A warm environment is essential when working with

dough that requires rising, proofing, or fermentation. A proofing box or proofer creates an optimal temperature and humidity-controlled space for the dough to grow consistently. This is particularly useful during winter when room temperatures may be more relaxed, ensuring that yeast-based recipes achieve the desired results.

In the world of Christmas baking, where the presentation

is as important as the taste, investing in decorative molds and stencils adds an extra layer of creativity. From intricately shaped cake pans to holiday-themed stencils for dusting powdered sugar, these tools elevate the visual appeal of festive treats, turning them into edible works of art.

For those who enjoy the efficiency of multitasking, a versatile food processor becomes an invaluable asset in the Christmas baking kitchen. From quickly chopping nuts to blending ingredients for pie crusts, a food processor streamlines preparation and saves time, allowing bakers to focus on the creative aspects of their recipes.

A selection of seasonal spices is a must to add a touch of warmth and aroma to holiday baking. Cinnamon, nutmeg, cloves, and ginger are classic Christmas spices that infuse treats with the nostalgic flavors of the season. A dedicated spice grinder ensures the freshness of ground spices, enhancing the baked goods' overall quality.

In recent years, technological advancements have introduced innovative kitchen gadgets catering to specific Christmas baking aspects. Digital temperature-controlled chocolate melters simplify the process of working with chocolate, ensuring smooth and perfectly tempered results. These gadgets are convenient when dipping cookies, creating chocolate decorations, or coating truffles.

When precision and consistency are paramount, a kitchen torch provides the finishing touch to sure desserts. From caramelizing the sugar atop a crème brûlée to adding a golden hue to the meringue, a kitchen torch allows for controlled and even browning, enhancing both the visual appeal and flavor of the final creations.

In conclusion, the must-have kitchen gadgets for Christmas baking form a comprehensive toolkit that empowers bakers to unleash their creativity and achieve stellar results. From the foundational stand mixer to the intricate cookie cutters, each gadget plays a distinct role in streamlining tasks, ensuring accuracy, and enhancing the overall baking experience. As the holiday season approaches, these essential tools become the companions that transform a humble kitchen into a festive workshop, where the magic of Christmas baking comes to life.

Exploring Unique Ingredients for Festive Delights

The magic of festive delights lies in the artful preparation, joy, full indulgence, and the unique ingredients that transform ordinary recipes into extraordinary culinary creations. As the holiday season approaches, the kitchen becomes a canvas for exploration, where bakers venture beyond the conventional pantry staples to discover and experiment with ingredients that impart distinct flavors, textures, and aromas to festive treats.

One quintessential ingredient defining the festive season is the warm, aromatic embrace of seasonal spices. With its sweet and woody notes, Cinnamon takes center stage, infusing everything from cookies to pies with a comforting essence. Nutmeg hints of earthiness, while cloves contribute a spicy and slightly sweet undertone. Ginger brings a zesty kick to baked goods, completing the quartet of spices that form the backbone of holiday treats. The artful combination of these spices transforms ordinary doughs and batters into festive wonders that evoke the season's spirit.

Beyond the familiar spices, including citrus infusions, it introduces freshness and brightness to festive delights. Oranges, lemons, and even grapefruits lend their zest and juice to myriad recipes, from cookies to cakes. The citrusy notes cut through the richness of butter and sugar, creating a harmonious balance that tantalizes the taste buds. Candied citrus peels, a delightful addition to fruitcakes and cookies, contribute flavor and lend a visually appealing texture to these festive confections.

Nuts and seeds, with their rich textures and nutty flavors, play a crucial role in elevating the complexity of festive treats. With their buttery richness, Pecans find their way into pies and pralines. Almonds, whether ground into flour or used whole, bring a delightful crunch to cookies and cakes. With their earthy undertones, walnuts pair perfectly with cinnamon and chocolate, adding depth to holiday recipes. Seeds, such as poppy and sesame seeds, contribute a unique texture and subtle nuttiness to various baked goods.

Dried fruits, a staple in festive baking, offer a concentrated burst of sweetness and chewiness. Raisins, sultanas, and currants find their way into fruitcakes and bread puddings, infusing them with pockets of succulent sweetness. Cranberries, with their vibrant hue and tartness, add a festive touch to cookies and scones. When chopped and incorporated into recipes, apricots, figs, and dates impart a delightful chewiness and a concentrated sweetness that enhances the overall flavor profile of festive treats.

The world of festive delights expands by introducing spirits and liqueurs into the baking repertoire. From the classic rum-soaked fruitcake to bourbon-infused chocolate truffles, these alcoholic additions bring depth, complexity, and a touch of sophistication to holiday treats. The interplay between the warmth of spirits and the sweetness of baked goods creates a harmonious marriage of flavors, often reminiscent of traditional holiday libations.

For those who seek to infuse a touch of international flair into their festive creations, exploring exotic flours and grains opens up a world of culinary possibilities. For instance, almond flour and coconut flour provide gluten-free alternatives that bring a distinct nuttiness and moisture to cookies and cakes. Ancient grains such as spelled and kamut introduce unique textures and nutritional benefits to holiday recipes, appealing to those with adventurous palates and dietary preferences.

The fragrant world of floral and herbal infusions introduces a layer of sophistication to festive baking. With its delicate aroma, lavender pairs beautifully with lemon in cookies and shortbreads. Rosemary, often associated with savory dishes, lends a surprising depth of flavor to sweet treats like olive oil cakes and sugar cookies. Edible flowers, such as pansies and violets, add a touch of elegance to desserts and bring floral notes that elevate the sensory experience of festive delights.

Chocolate, a perennial favorite in baking, unveils its universe of diversity and complexity. Exploring single-origin chocolates beyond the familiar sweetened chocolate bars introduces a spectrum of flavors, from fruity and tangy to deep and earthy. The percentage of cocoa in chocolate contributes to its intensity, allowing bakers to tailor the richness of their creations. Whether incorporating dark chocolate chunks into cookies or crafting a velvety ganache for cakes, the nuances of chocolate deepen the sensory experience of festive treats.

In the era of dietary diversity, the exploration of dairy alternatives has become a significant aspect of festive baking. Coconut, almond, and oat milk offer lactose-free options that bring unique flavors and textures to recipes. Baking with non-dairy substitutes extends the joy of festive treats to those with dietary restrictions, ensuring everyone can partake in the seasonal indulgence.

The quest for sweetness takes a nuanced turn, exploring sweeteners beyond traditional sugar. Honey, with its distinct floral notes, adds a natural sweetness to cookies and glazes. With its rich and robust flavor, Maple syrup complements the earthy tones of nuts and spices. Agave nectar, a low-glycemic alternative, imparts a mild sweetness that harmonizes with various festive ingredients. The diverse array of sweeteners allows bakers to tailor the level and character of sweetness in their holiday creations.

As the boundaries of culinary exploration expand, incorporating international flavors becomes a delightful venture in festive baking. Drawing inspiration from global cuisines introduces unique ingredients and techniques that infuse a sense of wanderlust into holiday treats. From cardamom-spiced cookies inspired by Indian flavors to anise-scented treats reminiscent of Mediterranean traditions, the fusion of global influences transforms the kitchen into a culinary passport for festive exploration.

In the spirit of unleashing creativity, the combination of unexpected and unconventional ingredients emerges as a trend in festive baking. The marriage of sweet and savory, such as bacon-infused chocolate truffles or rosemary-infused shortbread, challenges traditional notions and surprises the palate. Adventurous bakers enjoy experimenting with ingredients like matcha powder, black sesame seeds, or savory spices like cayenne pepper to create unexpected twists on classic holiday treats.

The celebration of festive delights extends beyond the kitchen, embracing the art of presentation and packaging. For instance, edible gold and silver leaf add a touch of luxury to desserts and chocolates. Elegant packaging, from ornate boxes to festive ribbons, transforms treats into cherished gifts, reflecting the spirit of giving during the holiday season.

In conclusion, exploring unique ingredients for festive delights is an enriching journey that transforms baking into a culinary adventure. From the familiar warmth of seasonal spices to the exotic allure of international flavors, each ingredient contributes its essence to the symphony of festive treats. As bakers venture beyond the ordinary, they discover a world of creativity, innovation, and sensory delight, elevating holiday baking into a cherished tradition that satisfies the sweet tooth and captivates the imagination. In exploring unique ingredients, the magic of festive delights truly comes to life, inviting everyone to savor the holiday season's joy and abundance.

CHAPTER III

Classic Christmas Cookies

Sugar Cookies and Royal Icing Masterclass

Embarking on the enchanting journey of creating sugar cookies adorned with intricate royal icing designs is akin to stepping into a culinary masterclass, where the artistry of baking meets the precision of decorating. Sugar cookies, with their delicate texture and buttery flavor, serve as the canvas for edible works of art that capture the spirit of celebration and creativity. The process involves mastering the foundational sugar cookie recipe and delving into the world of royal icing. This versatile and glossy medium transforms cookies into festive masterpieces.

The foundation of any sugar cookie and royal icing masterclass begins with the perfect sugar cookie recipe. This classic dough, comprised of flour, sugar, butter, and eggs, forms the basis for creating cookies with a tender crumb and buttery richness. The key lies in achieving the right balance of ingredients, ensuring that the dough is well-chilled for easy handling and that the baked cookies maintain their distinct shape and flavor. The sugar cookie dough is a blank canvas, awaiting the decorative touch of royal icing.

Royal icing, a mixture of confectioners' sugar, egg whites or meringue powder, and water is the magical medium that transforms sugar cookies into edible works of art. The key to successful royal icing is consistency in various decorating techniques. A thicker consistency is ideal for outlining and creating defined borders, while a thinner consistency allows flooding and quickly filling more significant areas. Adding meringue powder provides stability and ensures the icing sets to a smooth and glossy finish.

One of the essential skills in the Sugar Cookie and Royal Icing masterclass is the art of flooding. Flooding involves using a thin royal icing consistency to fill the interior of an outlined cookie shape, creating a smooth and even surface. This technique is the foundation for creating vibrant and colorful backgrounds on sugar cookies. Bakers learn to control the icing flow, ensuring it reaches the edges without overflowing, resulting in beautifully flooded cookies ready for additional layers of decoration.

The masterclass extends to the art of piping intricate details using royal icing. From delicate lines and swirls to complex patterns and designs, piping allows bakers to unleash their creativity on the sugar cookie canvas. Using piping bags fitted with various tips, each serving a specific purpose, becomes a skill that evolves with practice. Bakers learn to control the pressure applied to the piping bag, creating thin lines for outlining and thicker lines for decorative elements. The precision of piping brings festive characters, intricate snowflakes, and personalized messages to life on the sugar cookies.

Coloring royal icing becomes a vibrant aspect of the masterclass as bakers experiment with gel or powder food coloring to achieve a spectrum of hues. Understanding color theory and the interplay of shades allows bakers to create visually appealing and harmonious designs. From traditional reds and greens for Christmas to pastel hues for springtime celebrations, the versatility of royal icing coloration enhances the festive spirit of sugar cookies.

Textures and patterns add depth and visual interest to sugar cookies, and the masterclass includes techniques such as marbling, stenciling, and brush embroidery. Marbling involves blending different colored icings to create a swirled or marble-like effect, adding a touch of elegance to the cookies. Stenciling allows bakers to apply intricate designs using powdered sugar or edible color spray, resulting in beautifully patterned cookies. Brush embroidery, a technique borrowed from traditional embroidery involves using a fine brush to create delicate textured patterns on the flooded royal icing surface.

The sugar cookie and royal icing masterclass also explores the art of layering and dimension. Bakers create multi-dimensional designs that captivate the eye by allowing each layer of icing to dry before adding subsequent details. Dimensional effects, such as raised piping or the addition of edible embellishments like sprinkles or edible pearls, elevate the visual appeal of sugar cookies, transforming them into edible works of art.

Texture plays a significant role in the sensory experience of sugar cookies, and the masterclass extends to techniques like flooding with sanding sugar or applying a royal icing glaze. Sanding sugar adds a delightful crunch and shimmer to the surface of flooded areas, creating a contrast in texture. A royal icing glaze, achieved by thinning the icing to a pourable consistency, results in a smooth and glossy surface that enhances sugar cookies' flavor and visual appeal.

The final stage of the masterclass involves the art of presentation and packaging. Sugar cookies, meticulously decorated and expertly crafted, become cherished gifts and festive centerpieces. The delicate cookies are often arranged in decorative boxes adorned with festive ribbons or personalized tags. The packaging not only preserves the freshness of the cookies but also transforms them into tokens of joy and appreciation, ready to be shared and savored during the holiday season.

As bakers embark on the sugar cookie and royal icing masterclass, they discover that the journey extends beyond the kitchen. It becomes a celebration of creativity, a journey of skill refinement, and an exploration of the joyful intersection of baking and artistry. The art of creating sugar cookies with royal icing transcends the realm of culinary delight, transforming each cookie into a miniature masterpiece that embodies the festive spirit and the joy of sharing edible works of art with loved ones.

The sugar cookie and royal icing masterclass is not just a lesson in baking; it's an invitation to embark on a culinary adventure where every cookie becomes a canvas for edible joy and celebration.

Gingerbread Creations: From Houses to Men

The allure of gingerbread transcends its role as a humble holiday treat; it transforms into a medium of artistic expression, inviting both novice bakers and seasoned confectioners to embark on a creative journey. From the quaint charm of gingerbread houses adorned with snowy icing to the whimsical personalities of gingerbread men, the art of gingerbread creations encompasses a broad spectrum of festive delights. This edible canvas, born from molasses, spices, and the alchemy of baking, has become a beloved symbol of the holiday season, synonymous with warmth, tradition, and the joy of edible craftsmanship.

The gingerbread dough is at the heart of any gingerbread creation—a magical concoction of flour, molasses, sugar, and spices. The signature blend of ginger, cinnamon, cloves, and nutmeg infuses the dough with a heady aroma that instantly evokes the spirit of the holidays. Creating the perfect gingerbread dough is an art, requiring precision in measurements and patience in the chilling process. When rolled out and baked, the resulting dough becomes the foundation for a myriad of gingerbread creations.

With their quaint charm and intricate details, gingerbread houses stand as the quintessential expression of gingerbread artistry. Constructing a gingerbread house involves precision in cutting and assembling the baked gingerbread panels. Once secured with royal icing "glue," the walls and roof become the canvas for a winter wonderland of decorations. Icing piped along the edges mimics snow-covered rooftops, and candy embellishments—from gumdrops to candy canes—transform the structure into a whimsical abode. The art of decorating a gingerbread house is an immersive experience where creativity knows no bounds. Whether inspired by classic architectural designs or whimsical fairy tales, each gingerbread house becomes a unique masterpiece that captures the season's magic.

Beyond houses, the world of gingerbread extends to the delightful realm of gingerbread men. These charming, human-shaped cookies become the perfect canvas for edible personalities. Armed with piping bags of colorful royal icing, bakers bring these gingerbread figures to life. Each gingerbread man becomes a miniature work of art adorned with sugary smiles, buttons, and festive attire. The art of decorating gingerbread men allows endless creativity, from traditional holiday motifs to personalized details that reflect the baker's imagination. With their endearing charm, gingerbread men add a touch of whimsy to holiday gatherings and serve as edible ambassadors of the festive spirit.

Gingerbread creations also encompass a variety of other forms, from animals and trees to ornaments and festive scenes. The versatility of gingerbread dough, coupled with the artistic possibilities of royal icing, transforms holiday baking into an edible art exhibition. Gingerbread animals, such as reindeer and polar bears, take shape with the careful use of cookie cutters and imaginative detailing. Gingerbread trees, adorned with edible ornaments and a dusting of powdered sugar "snow," become elegant centerpieces for holiday tables. Edible ornaments crafted from gingerbread add a personal touch to holiday décor, infusing homes with the sweet fragrance of the season.

The process of creating gingerbread creations goes beyond the aesthetic appeal—it becomes a sensory experience that engages sight, smell, and taste. The warm spices permeate the kitchen as the gingerbread dough bakes, filling the air with the nostalgic fragrance of holiday cheer. The tactile pleasure of rolling out the dough and cutting intricate shapes adds a hands-on element to the creative process. The anticipation builds as the gingerbread bakes to golden perfection, and the kitchen transforms into a holiday workshop brimming with festive possibilities.

The art of gingerbread creation is not limited to the confines of home kitchens; it extends to grand displays and competitions that showcase the skill and creativity of professional bakers and enthusiasts alike. Gingerbread festivals and contests draw participants from all walks of life, inviting them to push the boundaries of edible artistry. Elaborate gingerbread villages, towering castles, and whimsical scenes come to life, capturing the imagination of onlookers and celebrating the limitless possibilities of gingerbread as a medium of edible creativity.

Gingerbread festivals often feature expansive displays beyond individual creations, creating immersive visitor experiences. The scale of these displays ranges from life-sized gingerbread structures to intricate miniature worlds. The artistic ingenuity showcased at these festivals reflects the diversity of gingerbread as an art form, from traditional designs that pay homage to classic fairy tales to contemporary, avant-garde interpretations that push the boundaries of what is possible with edible materials.

The tradition of gingerbread creations extends globally, with various cultures adding their unique twists to this festive art form. In Sweden, gingerbread houses, known as pepparkakshus, are integral to holiday celebrations. Intricate gingerbread churches inspired by historic stave churches are crafted meticulously in Norway. In the United Kingdom, gingerbread biscuits, often shaped as stars and decorated with white icing, are a cherished part of the Christmas tea tradition. The art of gingerbread transcends cultural boundaries, uniting people in the universal joy of edible creativity.

As the holiday season unfolds, gingerbread creations become edible works of art and cherished traditions passed down through generations. Families gather in kitchens, rolling out gingerbread dough, piping royal icing, and adorning creations with candies and decorations. Creating gingerbread houses and men becomes a shared experience, fostering moments of connection, laughter, and the joy of collaborative creativity.

Gingerbread creations also play a role in festive storytelling, weaving edible tales that capture the season's magic. Gingerbread houses evoke memories of fairy tales like "Hansel and Gretel," where enchanted homes made of sweets come to life. With their charming personalities, Gingerbread men become characters in the festive narrative, adding a touch of whimsy to holiday storytelling. The edible artistry of gingerbread becomes a means of sharing delicious treats and enchanting stories that accompany them.

In conclusion, the world of gingerbread creations celebrates edible artistry that transforms baking into a festive adventure. From the charm of gingerbread houses to the endearing personalities of gingerbread men, each creation becomes a canvas for imagination and creativity. The art of gingerbread extends beyond the kitchen, captivating the senses and fostering traditions that bridge cultures and generations. As gingerbread ovens warm and royal icing flows, the holiday season is infused with the magic of gingerbread—an art form that delights, inspires, and brings joy to all who partake in its sweet and whimsical creations.

CHAPTER IV

Decadent Cakes and Cupcakes

Perfecting the Art of Yule Log Cakes

The Yule log, or Bûche de Noël, is a timeless emblem of festive indulgence, embodying the spirit of celebration and the culinary artistry that defines holiday baking. This iconic dessert, shaped to resemble a log traditionally burned in the hearth during the Yuletide season, has become a canvas for pastry chefs and home bakers to showcase their creativity and skill. Perfecting the art of Yule log cakes involves a harmonious dance of flavors, textures, and aesthetics, resulting in a showstopping centerpiece that captivates the eye and delights the palate.

At the heart of any Yule log masterpiece lies the sponge cake, a delicate and airy canvas that serves as the foundation for the log's enchanting design. The sponge cake, typically a genoise, is characterized by its light texture and ability to absorb flavorful syrups or liqueurs. Achieving the perfect sponge cake involves whipping eggs and sugar to a ribbon-like consistency, creating the ideal structure for a tender and moist crumb. Adding flour, often folded gently to preserve the cake's airy quality, ensures a stable yet ethereal foundation for the layers.

Flavor infusions play a pivotal role in elevating the sponge cake to a level of culinary sophistication. From subtle hints of vanilla to bold notes of chocolate or coffee, the choice of flavor sets the tone for the entire Yule log experience. Liqueurs or syrups brushed onto the cake layers enhance moisture and introduce complementary or contrasting flavors. The art of flavor balancing becomes a central tenet of Yule log perfection as bakers navigate the interplay of sweetness, richness, and the nuanced subtleties of chosen flavor profiles.

Layering becomes a critical element of constructing the Yule log, with each stratum contributing to the overall textural experience. Creamy fillings, ranging from classic buttercream to decadent ganache, create a luscious interplay with the sponge cake layers. The art of layering extends beyond flavor to visual appeal, with contrasting colors and textures giving the Yule log its characteristic depth. It is rolled into a cylindrical shape, and the log forms its layers, becoming a visual tapestry that sets the stage for artistic embellishments.

The exterior of the Yule log is a canvas for creative expression, where the art of cake decorating comes to life. Ganache, buttercream, or frosting becomes the medium through which the Yule log's bark-like texture is replicated, capturing the essence of its rustic inspiration. The use of a serrated knife or fork creates lifelike patterns, adding a touch of realism to the edible log. The meticulous attention to detail, from the subtle grooves to the irregularities reminiscent of natural bark, transforms the Yule log into a visual masterpiece that pays homage to its forest-inspired origins.

Embellishments, such as meringue mushrooms, marzipan decorations, or edible flowers, add a whimsical and festive touch to the Yule log. These decorative elements enhance the visual appeal and contribute to the overall sensory experience. The meringue mushrooms, delicately crafted to resemble their woodland counterparts, introduce a crisp texture and a hint of sweetness. Marzipan decorations, shaped into leaves or berries, offer a delightful almond flavor that complements the other components. Edible flowers, carefully chosen for their visual impact and subtle floral notes, add a touch of elegance to the Yule log's presentation.

The final flourish in perfecting the art of Yule log cakes is the finishing touch of powdered sugar "snow" or a dusting of cocoa, creating a winter wonderland effect that enhances the festive ambiance. The Yule log, now transformed into an edible work of art, takes its place as the centerpiece of holiday gatherings, a symbol of joy, indulgence, and craftsmanship that defines the culinary traditions of the season.

Beyond its visual and gustatory appeal, the Yule log carries a rich history rooted in ancient traditions. It was burning a Yule log as a symbolic gesture of warmth and light that dates back to pagan celebrations, where the log represented the rejuvenation of the sun during the winter solstice. As Christianity spread, the Yule log became intertwined with Christmas traditions, evolving into an edible form that pays homage to the enduring symbolism of the log as a source of comfort and celebration during the year's darkest days.

As a contemporary expression of this ancient tradition, the Yule log cake has become a global phenomenon, celebrated in various forms and flavors across cultures. The Bûche de Noël is a staple of holiday celebrations in France, with patisseries showcasing elaborate and artistic interpretations. In Sweden, the tradition of the "Julgransplundring" involves the symbolic devouring of a Yule log cake during the Christmas tree-plundering festivities. Each culture brings flair to the art of Yule log cakes, reflecting local ingredients, flavors, and artistic sensibilities.

The art of perfecting Yule log cakes is not confined to professional pastry kitchens; it has also become a cherished tradition in home kitchens. Families gather, don aprons, and embark on the joyous journey of crafting their Yule log, infusing the process with the warmth of shared creativity. Children and adults participate in the decorating festivities, adding their personal touches and creating memories that transcend the boundaries of taste and texture.

As the Yule log takes its place on the holiday table, it becomes more than a dessert; it becomes a symbol of togetherness, tradition, and the enduring magic of the season. The artistry in perfecting Yule log cakes goes beyond the technical aspects of baking and decorating; it encapsulates the spirit of celebration and the joy of creating something beautiful and delicious to be shared with loved ones. With its rich history, cultural significance, and culinary artistry, the Yule log continues to be a timeless expression of the festive season, embodying the magic of the holidays in every slice.

Festive Cupcake Decorating Techniques

The art of cupcake decorating during the festive season transcends mere culinary expression; it becomes a delightful fusion of creativity, taste, and visual appeal. Festive cupcakes serve as miniature canvases for bakers to showcase their artistry, infusing the joy and spirit of the holidays into each delectable creation. From whimsical winter wonderlands to elegant designs inspired by traditional holiday motifs, the techniques employed in decorating festive cupcakes are as diverse as the celebrations they adorn.

At the core of festive cupcake decorating lies the foundation—the cupcake itself. This miniature cake serves as the canvas upon which the festive magic unfolds. Whether it's a classic vanilla, a rich chocolate, or a spiced gingerbread, the flavor of the cupcake sets the tone for the entire decorating experience. The choice of flavor can evoke nostalgic memories of holiday treats or introduce new and inventive twists, capturing the essence of the season in every bite.

Texture plays a crucial role in cupcake decorating, and the art of achieving the perfect crumb becomes a fundamental skill. Moist and tender cupcakes provide a delectable contrast to the creamy frostings and fillings that will adorn them. The balance of ingredients, meticulous mixing, and careful baking all contribute to the desired texture, making each bite a delight. With its moist crumb and flavorful profile, the festive cupcake becomes the perfect canvas ready to be adorned with edible art.

Frosting becomes the palette with which bakers bring their festive cupcake visions to life. The choice of frosting—a classic buttercream, a velvety cream cheese, or a glossy ganache—adds a layer of richness and indulgence to the cupcakes. The art of frosting application involves precision, whether using a spatula for a rustic swirl or a piping bag fitted with a decorative tip for intricate designs. The texture and consistency of the frosting contribute not only to the visual appeal but also to the overall sensory experience of the festive cupcake.

Color plays a starring role in festive cupcake decorating, with the hues chosen reflecting the cheerful palette of the season. From traditional reds and greens to icy blues and sparkling gold, the colors used in decorating cupcakes evoke the holiday spirit. Carefully mixed into frostings, gel, or powder food coloring allows precise color customization. In contrast, natural ingredients such as matcha powder or beet juice offer vibrant alternatives for those seeking a more organic approach. The use of color extends beyond the frosting to decorative elements, from sprinkles and edible pearls to festive cupcake liners that enhance the visual appeal.

Texture and dimension come to life with edible embellishments, transforming festive cupcakes into edible works of art. Texture incorporates chopped nuts, coconut flakes, or crushed candy canes to add crunch and visual interest. Edible pearls, sanding sugar, or shimmering dust introduce a touch of glamour, creating cupcakes that glisten and sparkle like holiday ornaments. Combining textures and dimensions adds a dynamic quality to festive cupcakes, making them visually enticing and tempting to the senses.

One of the hallmark techniques in festive cupcake decorating is the art of piping intricate designs. Piping involves using a pastry bag with various tips to create patterns, rosettes, swirls, and other decorative elements. The precision required for piping elevates cupcakes from simple treats to edible art forms. Bakers may pipe holiday motifs like snowflakes, holly leaves, or Christmas trees, or they may opt for more abstract designs that showcase their creativity. The versatility of piping techniques allows for endless possibilities, from elegant and refined to whimsical and playful.

Fondant, a pliable sugar paste, offers festive cupcake decorating possibilities. Rolled out and draped over cupcakes, fondant provides a smooth and flawless canvas for intricate designs. Working with fondant involves precision in rolling, cutting, and shaping to achieve desired forms. Fondant allows for creating sculpted toppers, themed figurines, or even edible holiday scenes that transform cupcakes into edible works of art. Its versatility in color, shape, and texture adds a sophisticated touch to festive cupcakes, making them stand out as both visually stunning and delicious.

The marbling technique introduces a touch of artistic flair to festive cupcakes, creating a visually captivating effect. Marbling involves swirling together multiple colors of frosting or batter to achieve a mesmerizing pattern reminiscent of marble stone. In cupcakes, this technique can be applied to both the frosting and the cake itself, resulting in a beautiful interplay of colors. Marbled cupcakes become miniature masterpieces that add an element of surprise and sophistication to holiday dessert tables.

Festive cupcake decorating extends beyond the visual to incorporate flavors and fillings that delight the taste buds. Filling cupcakes with jams, curds, or ganache introduces layers of flavor that complement the chosen cake and frosting. The art of filling cupcakes involves creating a well in the center of the baked cupcake and adding a dollop of the chosen filling before sealing it with an additional layer of cake. The burst of flavor that comes with each bite adds a delightful element of surprise, transforming festive cupcakes into a multi-sensory experience.

The holiday season provides ample inspiration for festive cupcake themes, allowing bakers to tell edible stories through their creations. From classic Christmas symbols like candy canes, ornaments, and stockings to winter wonderland scenes with snowflakes and icicles, thematic cupcake decorating sparks joy and nostalgia. Cupcake toppers, crafted from edible materials like fondant or royal icing, serve as miniature works of art that bring holiday tales to life. The artistry in thematic cupcake decorating goes beyond technical skill; it consists of capturing the season's essence and translating it into edible delights.

Festive cupcake decorating is not confined to professional bakers; it has also become a cherished tradition in home kitchens. Families come together to bake and decorate cupcakes, creating moments of joy, laughter and shared creativity. Children eagerly join the decorating festivities, adding their personal touches and infusing the process with the boundless imagination of youth. Decorating festive cupcakes becomes a shared experience that extends the warmth and joy of the holiday season beyond the dining table.

In conclusion, the art of festive cupcake decorating is a celebration of creativity, taste, and visual appeal. From the choice of flavors and textures to the meticulous techniques of frosting, piping, and embellishing, each element contributes to the overall artistry of festive cupcakes. Beyond their culinary appeal, festive cupcakes become edible works of art that capture the holiday season's joy, spirit, and nostalgia. As these miniature masterpieces grace dessert tables and bring smiles to faces, they embody the essence of celebration and the magic of edible art during the festive season.

CHAPTER V

Pies and Tarts for the Holidays

Crafting the Ultimate Mince Pie

Crafting the ultimate mince pie is an art steeped in tradition, a culinary endeavor that transcends mere baking to become a cherished symbol of the festive season. These miniature delights, with their golden crusts cradling a rich and spiced filling, evoke the warmth and nostalgia of holiday gatherings. Perfecting the mince pie extends beyond mere ingredients and measurements; it encompasses a delicate dance of flavors, textures, and the meticulous craft of pastry-making. As the aroma of cinnamon, nutmeg, and dried fruits wafts through the kitchen, the artistry of crafting the ultimate mince pie unfolds, inviting both novice bakers and seasoned pastry enthusiasts to partake in this time-honored tradition.

At the heart of crafting the ultimate mince pie lies the essence of the filling—a symphony of flavors that harmonize to create a luscious and aromatic center. Contrary to its name, traditional mince pie filling doesn't actually contain meat. Instead, it is a delightful melange of dried fruits, spices, suet, and sometimes a splash of brandy or rum for a festive kick. The art of crafting the perfect filling lies in achieving a balance that marries sweetness with a subtle richness, ensuring each bite is a journey through layers of nuanced flavors. The mix of raisins, currants, sultanas, and candied peel provides sweetness and depth, while the suet contributes a velvety richness that binds the ingredients into a cohesive, flavorful blend. The judicious addition of spices— cinnamon, nutmeg, and allspice—infuses the filling with the quintessential warmth and aroma of the holiday season.

The choice of pastry is a pivotal aspect in crafting the ultimate mince pie, and traditional shortcrust pastry reigns supreme in this culinary tradition. The delicate balance of flour, butter, and a touch of sugar creates a pastry that crumbles with each bite, providing the perfect contrast to the rich and spiced filling. Pastry-making involves a keen understanding of the ingredients and their proportions. Chilled to the right consistency, butter is meticulously rubbed into the flour until the mixture resembles fine breadcrumbs. A sprinkle of cold water is then added, and the dough is gently kneaded to form a smooth, cohesive ball. The key lies in handling the pastry carefully, ensuring it remains relaxed and pliable, allowing easy rolling and shaping.

Crafting the perfect pastry for mince pies involves the art of rolling—creating a thin and even sheet that will encase the flavorful filling. The skill lies in achieving the right thickness and ensuring that the pastry retains its delicate texture. Using a floured surface and a well-chilled rolling pin helps maintain the pastry's integrity, preventing it from becoming brutal or overworked. The art of cutting out circles, each destined to cradle a spoonful of mincemeat, adds a touch of precision to the process. The ultimate goal is to create a pastry shell that is sturdy enough to hold the filling yet tender enough to yield a gentle bite.

The assembly of mince pies involves a ceremonial dance of pastry circles and aromatic filling, each element carefully arranged to create the perfect bite-sized indulgence. A dollop of mincemeat, rich with the flavors of dried fruits and spices, is nestled into the center of each pastry round. The art of sealing the pies involves a delicate balance—ensuring that the edges are crimped with precision to encase the filling securely while allowing for the golden beauty of the pastry to shine through. The process becomes a rhythmic dance of hands, a culinary expression of the holiday spirit taking shape in each handcrafted pie.

Baking the mince pies requires patience and a keen eye for detail. Achieving the perfect golden hue involves carefully balancing temperature and timing. A preheated oven ensures the pastry begins to crisp and brown when it meets the heat. The aromas that waft through the kitchen during the baking process are a sensory testament to the culmination of flavors within the oven's confines. The ultimate goal is a batch of mince pies with a golden-brown crust, an enticing aroma, and a promise of decadent delight.

The finishing touch to crafting the ultimate mince pie often involves dusting powdered sugar or a light glaze to enhance the visual appeal. This simple yet elegant addition adds a festive charm, transforming the pies into miniature works of art that are as delightful to behold as they are to savor. The artistry involved in presenting mince pies extends beyond their culinary allure; it transforms them into a centerpiece for holiday gatherings, a symbol of tradition, and a gesture of hospitality.

Beyond the craft of mince pie making lies the rich tapestry of tradition and folklore woven around these delectable treats. The origins of mince pies can be traced back to medieval England, where they were initially filled with minced meat, suet, and spices—a savory concoction influenced by Middle Eastern flavors. Over the centuries, the recipe evolved to incorporate sweetened dried fruits, making them more reminiscent of the mince pies we know today. The association of mince pies with Christmas is steeped in centuries-old traditions, where the spices and flavors symbolize the holiday season's warmth and festivity.

The symbolism of mince pies extends beyond their ingredients and baking process to encompass cultural and familial traditions. In the United Kingdom, it is customary to make a wish while consuming the first mince pie of the season, a practice believed to bring good luck. The act of leaving out mince pies for Santa Claus on Christmas Eve is a tradition observed in many households, an offering of gratitude for the joy and magic of the season. Mince pies become a thread that weaves through generations, connecting the present to the past and creating a tapestry of shared memories and festive rituals.

As mince pies take their place on festive tables, they become more than a dessert; they become an edible embodiment of tradition, heritage, and the enduring magic of the holidays. The craft of creating the ultimate mince pie is a celebration of flavors and textures, a journey into the heart of culinary artistry that transcends the act of baking to become a cherished tradition. Each bite is a symphony of spices, a dance of textures, and a connection to the rich history and folklore surrounding these iconic treats. As families gather and friends come together to share the season's joy, the ultimate mince pie becomes a sweet and savory ambassador of festive cheer. This edible masterpiece encapsulates the spirit of celebration and the magic of the holidays in every bite.

Fruitful Tarts: A Symphony of Flavors

The art of crafting fruitful tarts is a symphony of flavors, a culinary journey that transforms simple ingredients into a harmonious celebration of taste and texture. These delightful pastries, adorned with an array of fresh and vibrant fruits, are not merely desserts; they are edible canvases that showcase the natural sweetness of seasonal produce. Creating fruitful tarts involves a careful dance of pastry-making, filling preparation, and the artistic arrangement of fruits. This meticulous endeavor elevates the humble tart to a sophisticated and visually stunning dessert.

At the heart of any fruitful tart lies the foundation—the pastry crust. The choice of pastry is a critical element in tart-making, and a well-executed crust is the perfect canvas for the symphony of flavors. Pâte brisée, a classic French shortcrust pastry, is a popular choice for its delicate, crumbly texture that provides a subtle contrast to the richness of the filling and the juiciness of the fruits.

The art of pastry-making involves carefully blending flour, butter, sugar, and a touch of salt, creating a tender yet sturdy dough to hold the delectable filling. The pastry is then rolled out, draped over the tart pan, and baked to golden perfection—an artful process that requires precision and a delicate touch.

The filling of a fruitful tart is a celebration of flavors that marries the sweetness of fruits with the richness of a velvety custard or a silky pastry cream. The choice of filling complements and enhances the natural sweetness of the fruits, creating a balance that tantalizes the taste buds. A classic pastry cream made with eggs, sugar, milk, and vanilla, provides a luscious base that adds depth and creaminess to the tart. Alternatively, a frangipane filling crafted from ground almonds, sugar, and butter introduces a nutty richness that pairs beautifully with various fruits. Filling preparation involves layering flavors and textures, creating a cohesive blend that transforms each bite into a moment of pure indulgence.

The selection and arrangement of fruits become a visual and gustatory artistry in fruitful tart creation. Seasonal fruits, bursting with freshness and vibrant colors, take center stage as both the stars and the palette for the artistic presentation. Berries, stone fruits, citrus slices, and exotic varieties all find their place on the tart, creating a visually stunning mosaic of flavors. The art of arranging fruits involves a keen eye for color balance, texture variation, and understanding how each fruit contributes to the overall composition. The process becomes a creative expression that transforms the tart into an edible work of art, capturing the season's essence.

The layering of fruits on the tart becomes a symphony of tastes and textures. Juicy berries offer a burst of sweetness, while slices of peaches or apricots add a tender bite. Citrus segments contribute a zesty brightness, and kiwi or pineapple brings a tropical twist. The art of layering fruits involves thoughtful consideration of their flavors and textures, creating a delightful interplay that keeps each bite exciting and dynamic. The fruits, carefully arranged in concentric circles or artistic patterns, become a feast for the taste buds and a visual spectacle that adds to the allure of the tart.

The final touch in crafting fruitful tarts often involves a glaze or a dusting of powdered sugar, adding a finishing flourish that enhances the visual appeal. A simple apricot glaze, gently brushed over the fruits, imparts a glossy sheen that elevates the tart's appearance. Powdered sugar, sifted delicately over the fruits, adds a touch of elegance and a hint of sweetness. The art of finishing touches is a delicate balance—enhancing the natural beauty of the fruits without overpowering their flavors, creating a tart that is not only delicious but also a feast for the eyes.

The creation of fruitful tarts extends beyond the kitchen to encompass cultural and seasonal traditions. In France, the tarte aux fruits is a quintessential summer dessert, showcasing an abundance of fresh berries and stone fruits. In Italy, the crostata di frutta is a beloved treat during celebrations and special occasions, often featuring a medley of seasonal fruits atop a buttery crust. The art of making fruitful tarts becomes a cultural expression, a way of celebrating the bountiful harvests and the joy of communal gatherings.

Beyond their cultural significance, fruitful tarts embody the essence of seasonal flavors and the joy of indulging in nature's bounty. The artistry involved in their creation becomes a form of culinary storytelling, where each tart tells a tale of the changing seasons, the ripening of fruits, and the anticipation of the harvest. A summer tart may boast a vibrant array of berries and stone fruits, while an autumn tart may feature the rich flavors of apples, pears, and figs. The art of creating seasonally inspired tarts allows bakers to connect with the rhythms of nature, infusing each dessert with a sense of time and place.

Fruitful tarts are not limited to professional kitchens; they have become a popular and accessible creation in home kitchens as well. Tart-making becomes a joyous endeavor, inviting home bakers to experiment with flavors, colors, and arrangements. Families gather in kitchens, inspired by the seasonal produce, to craft their versions of fruitful tarts. Children eagerly join the process, arranging slices of fruits and contributing to the creative expression. Making fruitful tarts becomes a shared experience, fostering moments of connection and joy.

In conclusion, crafting fruitful tarts celebrates flavors, textures, and the visual beauty of seasonal fruits. Each element contributes to the overall symphony of taste and presentation, from the delicate pastry crust to the luscious filling and the artful arrangement of fruits. Fruitful tarts are more than desserts; they are edible works of art that capture the essence of the season and the joy of indulging in nature's bounty. As families and friends come together to savor each bite, fruitful tarts become a delightful expression of culinary artistry, a celebration of flavors that transcend the boundaries of taste to create a sensory experience that lingers in the memory.

CHAPTER VI

Holiday Bread and Rolls

Traditional Christmas Stollen Recipe

The traditional Christmas stollen is a revered masterpiece of festive baking, a culinary treasure that transcends generations and cultures. Originating from Germany, this iconic sweet bread has become synonymous with Christmas, gracing tables worldwide with its rich history and delectable flavor. Crafting a traditional Christmas stollen involves more than combining ingredients; it is a time-honored tradition, a labor of love that weaves together the warmth of the holiday spirit and the artistry of baking.

The dough is at the heart of the traditional Christmas stollen—a delicate and enriched bread that forms the foundation of this festive treat. Creating the perfect stollen dough requires carefully balancing flour, yeast, butter, sugar, and eggs. The yeast imparts a light and airy texture, while the butter and sugar contribute richness and sweetness. With their golden yolks, eggs enhance the dough's structure and add a velvety softness. The combination of these ingredients, mixed and kneaded with precision, results in a tender and indulgent dough— a canvas ready to embrace the flavors and textures of the festive season.

The soul of the traditional Christmas stollen lies in its filling—a symphony of fruits, nuts, and spices that infuse each slice with a burst of holiday joy. Raisins, currants, and candied citrus peels contribute sweetness and chewiness, while almonds or marzipan introduce a nutty richness. The art of creating the filling involves meticulously soaking the dried fruits in rum or brandy, infusing them with the season's essence. The spices, such as cinnamon, nutmeg, and cardamom, add warmth and complexity, creating a fragrant medley that evokes the spirit of Christmas.

The assembly of the stollen becomes a culinary dance, where the enriched dough is rolled out and carefully enveloped in the luscious filling. The shaping of the stollen involves a distinctive fold that resembles a rolled-up blanket, symbolizing the swaddling of the Christ child—a tradition rooted in the stollen's religious origins. The act of folding and shaping requires a deft hand and an understanding of the dough's elasticity, ensuring that each stollen perfectly balances bread and filling. As the loaves rest and rise, the anticipation builds, and the kitchen fills with the heavenly aroma of baking stollen.

Baking the stollen is a transformative process, where the loaves undergo a glorious metamorphosis in the oven. Achieving the perfect golden-brown crust involves carefully balancing temperature and timing. The loaves emerge, radiating warmth and fragrance, their surfaces adorned with a dusting of powdered sugar that mimics the winter snow—a visual reminder of the seasonal joy encapsulated in each slice. The act of baking becomes a ritual, a moment where the kitchen is filled with the scent of freshly baked bread and the magic of Christmas.

The final touch in the traditional Christmas stollen is a generous coating of melted butter, anointing each loaf with a golden sheen that adds to its decadence. The butter serves a dual purpose—enhancing the stollen's flavor and creating a protective seal that keeps the bread moist during its maturation. Traditionally, stollen is baked weeks before Christmas, allowing its flavors to meld and intensify over time. Patiently waiting for the stollen to mature becomes part of the tradition, building anticipation for the moment when it will finally be sliced and savored.

Beyond its delectable taste and fragrant aroma, the traditional Christmas stollen carries a rich cultural and historical significance tapestry. The stollen's roots trace back to Dresden, Germany, where it was first documented in the 15th century. Originally crafted with simple ingredients and intended as a dietary supplement during Advent fasting, the stollen has evolved over the centuries into a symbol of indulgence and celebration. Its association with Christmas is intertwined with the rich history of German holiday traditions, and today, the baking and sharing of stollen are cherished customs that extend beyond the borders of Germany.

Gifting a stollen during Christmas is a gesture of goodwill and camaraderie. Traditionally, the stollen is presented as a token of appreciation to friends, family, and neighbors. In Dresden, a grand Stollenfest is held annually, where a giant stollen, weighing several tons, is paraded through the city before being sliced and distributed to the crowd— a spectacle that embodies the communal spirit of the holiday season. Sharing stollen becomes a way of spreading joy and fostering connections, a tradition that resonates with the essence of Christmas.

The symbolism of the stollen extends beyond its physical form to encompass religious allegory. The folded shape of the stollen resembles the swaddling clothes in which the infant Jesus was wrapped, and the powdered sugar symbolizes the purity of Christ. The inclusion of dried fruits and nuts mirrors the offerings of the Three Wise Men, adding a layer of biblical significance to this festive bread. Consuming stollen becomes a communion with tradition, a moment where the sacred and the culinary converge.

Crafting a traditional Christmas stollen is not limited to professional bakers; it has also found a cherished place in home kitchens. Families combine to mix, knead, and shape the dough, infusing the process with laughter and shared joy. Children eagerly participate in the festive ritual, their hands dusted with flour as they help shape the stollen and eagerly await the moment when they can savor its sweet rewards. Making stollen becomes a bonding experience, a time when generations connect through the timeless art of baking.

In conclusion, the traditional Christmas stollen is more than a festive bread; it is a cultural treasure, a symbol of tradition, and a culinary masterpiece that embodies the spirit of Christmas. From the tender enriched dough to the fragrant filling and the meticulous shaping, each step in the stollen-making process is an act of love and craftsmanship. As families gather around tables to share slices of stollen, they partake in a tradition that transcends time, connecting them with this iconic Christmas treat's rich history and cultural significance. The traditional Christmas stollen is more than bread; it manifests the holiday spirit—a delicious reminder of the joy, warmth, and togetherness that define the Christmas season.

Pull-Apart Dinner Rolls for a Festive Feast

The allure of pull-apart dinner rolls is not merely confined to their delightful taste; it lies in the communal experience they bring to festive feasts. These small, fluffy creations, baked to golden perfection and arranged in a harmonious cluster, symbolize the spirit of sharing and togetherness inherent in celebratory gatherings. The journey of crafting pull-apart dinner rolls involves more than the amalgamation of flour, yeast, and butter; it is a culinary art form that transforms humble ingredients into a centerpiece for festive tables.

At the heart of pull-apart dinner rolls is the dough—an amalgamation of basic pantry staples that undergoes a magical metamorphosis in the hands of a skilled baker. Flour, yeast, sugar, butter, and a pinch of salt come together to create a supple, elastic dough and imbued with the promise of softness. The art of kneading the dough is a tactile experience, requiring a rhythmic motion that builds the gluten structure essential for the rolls' airy texture. Patience becomes a virtue as the dough undergoes fermentation, its yeasty aroma filling the kitchen with the promise of warm, freshly baked goodness.

The shaping of pull-apart dinner rolls involves a meticulous process that elevates them from mere dough balls to an enticing ensemble. Dividing the dough into uniform portions ensures consistency in both appearance and texture. The shaping technique, whether the classic round ball or a more intricate knot, adds a touch of artistry to each roll. The rolls are then nestled closely in a pan, their proximity during baking fostering a sense of connection and unity, setting the stage for the communal act of pulling them apart.

Baking the rolls is a transformative ritual that fills the kitchen with an irresistible aroma. Achieving the perfect golden-brown crust involves carefully balancing temperature and timing. As the rolls rise and expand in the oven, their individuality melds into a collective entity, each roll contributing to the pull-apart nature that makes them uniquely suited for communal sharing. The sight of a pan filled with golden, fragrant rolls is a harbinger of the joy and friendliness that awaits at the festive table.

Pulling apart dinner rolls transcends mere mechanics; it is a communal gesture that fosters a sense of camaraderie and shared enjoyment. Placed at the center of the table, the pan of pull-apart rolls becomes a focal point—a tactile invitation for diners to engage in the age-old ritual of breaking bread together. The act of tearing into the rolls, the soft crumb yielding to reveal the steam within, becomes a symbol of abundance and the simple pleasures of good food shared among loved ones.

Pull-apart dinner rolls are versatile canvases that can be customized to suit the theme and flavors of the festive feast. Adding herbs, such as rosemary or thyme, infuses the rolls with savory notes that complement a hearty holiday meal. For a touch of sweetness, a sprinkle of cinnamon sugar or a drizzle of honey transforms the rolls into a delightful accompaniment to festive brunches or desserts. The art of flavor customization allows bakers to showcase their creativity, adding a personal touch to this classic bread.

The presentation of pull-apart dinner rolls is an aesthetic endeavor that enhances the overall visual appeal of the festive table. The rolls, arranged in a decorative pattern or nestled in a festive wreath, become an edible centerpiece that captivates the eyes before tantalizing the taste buds. Adding seeds, such as sesame or poppy, creates a textured crust that adds visual interest and a subtle nuttiness to each bite. The art of presentation transforms pull-apart dinner rolls into edible art that elevates the dining experience.

Beyond their culinary appeal, pull-apart dinner rolls carry a symbolic significance deeply rooted in cultural and familial traditions. Breaking bread together has long been a universal symbol of communion and unity, a gesture that transcends language and cultural barriers. In many cultures, sharing bread signifies hospitality, generosity, and a shared sense of community. Pull-apart dinner rolls, with their portions neatly nestled together, embody this tradition, inviting diners to partake in a shared experience beyond mere eating.

The pull-apart dinner roll, while a quintessential feature of festive feasts, also has a place in everyday moments. Its charm is simple, making it suitable for casual family dinners and grand celebrations. The art of making pull-apart rolls can become a cherished family tradition, with generations coming together to pass down the tactile knowledge of dough-making and the shared joy of breaking bread. In this way, the humble pull-apart dinner roll becomes a vessel for transmitting culinary heritage and creating lasting memories.

The significance of pull-apart dinner rolls extends beyond cultural boundaries to encompass the universal themes of warmth, connection, and the joy of shared meals. In a world where breaking bread together holds a timeless allure, pull-apart dinner rolls are a testament to the enduring appeal of simple, communal pleasures. As they grace festive tables, these rolls become a side dish and a catalyst for the bonds that form when loved ones gather to celebrate, connect, and share in the season's abundance.

In conclusion, pull-apart dinner rolls are more than a

staple at festive feasts; they are a culinary art form that encapsulates the spirit of sharing and togetherness. From creating the dough to pulling it apart at the table, each step in the process celebrates craftsmanship and communal joy. As families and friends gather around festive tables, the humble pull-apart dinner roll symbolizes abundance, warmth, and the timeless tradition of breaking bread together. Its simplicity carries the weight of tradition, the joy of connection, and the enduring appeal of the communal act of sharing a meal.

CHAPTER VII

Sweet and Savory Pastries

Puff Pastry Wonders: From Mince Pies to Palmiers

The art of puff pastry transcends the boundaries of culinary technique to become a canvas for an array of delectable creations, ranging from the classic mince pies that grace holiday tables to the delicate palmiers that enchant dessert enthusiasts. Puff pastry, with its ethereal layers and buttery richness, is a testament to the marriage of precision and artistry in baking. Its origins, dating back centuries, speak to the enduring appeal of this flaky and versatile dough. At the same time, its varied applications showcase the breadth of creativity that can be achieved with a simple amalgamation of flour, butter, and water.

The lamination process is at the core of puff pastry's allure—an intricate dance of rolling, folding, and chilling that creates the ethereal layers synonymous with this dough. The foundation lies in a basic mixture of flour and water, enriched with a generous incorporation of butter through a series of folds. The dough is then rolled out, folded, and chilled repeatedly, allowing the layers to develop and the butter to create pockets of air during baking. The result is a pastry that shatters upon the touch, revealing a delicate network of flaky layers that beckon with each bite.

One of the quintessential uses of puff pastry during the festive season is the creation of mince pies; iconic treats embody the warmth and nostalgia of holiday gatherings. The rich, buttery layers of puff pastry provide the perfect vessel to cradle a spiced and fruity mincemeat filling. The juxtaposition of the crisp, golden crust and the sweet, aromatic mincemeat creates a symphony of textures and flavors. Steeped in tradition and folklore, mince pies carry the essence of Christmas, their very presence on the table evoking the spirit of celebration and shared joy.

Palmiers, also known as elephant ears or palm leaves, showcase a different facet of puff pastry's versatility. These delicate, heart-shaped treats are a study in simplicity, where the interplay of sugar and butter transforms the dough into a caramelized, crispy confection. The art of making palmiers lies in the precision of the sugar coating and the strategic folding of the dough to create the characteristic shape. The result is a pastry that is both visually stunning and irresistibly addictive—a testament to the transformative power of puff pastry in the hands of a skilled baker.

The magic of puff pastry extends beyond sweet creations to savory delights that grace brunch tables and cocktail parties alike. From elegant cheese straws to delicious pinwheels filled with herbs and cheese, the versatility of puff pastry shines through in its ability to effortlessly transition between the realms of sweet and savory. The buttery layers provide a perfect foil for savory fillings, creating appetizers and snacks that are as visually appealing as they are delicious. Puff pastry becomes a vehicle for culinary innovation, inviting chefs and home cooks alike to experiment with flavors and presentations.

The cultural significance of puff pastry is woven into the fabric of global cuisines, with each culture putting its unique spin on this versatile dough. In France, the birthplace of puff pastry, it is a cornerstone of classic pastries like the mille-feuille, where layers of puff pastry alternate with pastry cream to create a decadent dessert. The delicate croissants that grace French patisseries are a testament to the mastery of laminated dough, with each flaky layer showcasing the precision and skill of the baker. In Spain, the ensaimada takes puff pastry in a different direction, coiling the dough into a sweet, spiral pastry that is a beloved treat during festivals and celebrations.

The art of making puff pastry has been passed down through generations, with each baker adding their touch to this timeless technique. The journey from a simple mixture of flour, water, and butter to a golden, flaky masterpiece involves skill and a deep understanding of the alchemy at play. The incorporation of butter, a key ingredient in puff pastry, demands a delicate balance—too little, and the layers won't form; too much, and the pastry loses its crispness. The rolling and folding process requires patience and precision, with each turn contributing to developing the ethereal layers that make puff pastry a culinary marvel.

Puff pastry's cultural and historical roots can be traced

back to medieval Muslim Spain, where laminating dough with butter was likely introduced. With their advanced knowledge of agriculture and culinary arts, the Moors brought this technique to the Iberian Peninsula, where it gradually spread across Europe. The French, renowned for their pastry craftsmanship, refined and perfected the art of puff pastry, elevating it to new heights in patisserie. Over the centuries, puff pastry has become a cornerstone of sweet and savory dishes, its influence extending to kitchens worldwide.

In the modern culinary landscape, the convenience of commercially available puff pastry has made this once labor-intensive technique more accessible to home cooks. Ready-made sheets of puff pastry open up a world of possibilities, allowing even novice bakers to create impressive and delicious treats with minimal effort. The versatility of puff pastry invites experimentation, encouraging home cooks to explore sweet and savory applications, from tarts and turnovers to sausage rolls and delicious pinwheels.

Whether from scratch or using store-bought sheets,

making puff pastry celebrates craftsmanship and creativity. Bakers and cooks find joy in the transformative nature of puff pastry, where a humble mixture of ingredients evolves into a golden, flaky canvas for culinary expression. Layering, folding, and shaping become a therapeutic exercise, a meditative journey that culminates in the joy of savoring the finished creation.

As puff pastry graces tables worldwide, from the festive desserts of the holiday season to the elegant pastries enjoyed in sidewalk cafes, it becomes a conduit for shared experiences and cultural expression. The buttery layers, delicate textures, and rich flavors encapsulate the essence of celebration and indulgence. In its many forms, puff pastry embodies the alchemy of baking, where humble ingredients are transformed into edible wonders that captivate the senses and create lasting memories. Whether in a flaky mince pie evoking the coziness of Christmas or a palmier offering a delicate dance of sweetness on the tongue, puff pastry is a testament to the enduring magic of the culinary arts.

Savory Pastry Twists for Christmas Brunch

The allure of savory pastry twists during the festive season adds a layer of indulgence and creativity to the Christmas brunch spread. These delectable treats, with their flaky layers and flavorful fillings, embody the spirit of celebration and communal feasting. The artistry of crafting savory pastry twists goes beyond mere baking; it involves a symphony of flavors, textures, and visual appeal that transforms a simple pastry into a culinary centerpiece for holiday gatherings.

The versatile buttery pastry dough is at the core of savory pastry twists, a canvas that holds the promise of layers upon layers of flakiness. Whether crafted from scratch or sourced from the convenience of pre-made puff pastry sheets, the dough becomes the foundation for a savory exploration. Its transformation from a basic mixture of flour, water, and butter to a golden, crisp marvel is a testament to the alchemy of baking—a process that demands precision, patience, and a keen understanding of the interplay between ingredients.

Crafting the perfect savory pastry twist involves the delicate dance of layering and filling. Rolled out to a precise thickness, the dough becomes a blank slate waiting to be adorned with a tapestry of flavors. The filling, a harmonious blend of savory ingredients, is spread evenly over the dough—perhaps a mixture of cheeses, herbs, and cured meats for a classic twist or a medley of seasonal vegetables and spices for a festive touch. The layers are then folded and twisted, creating a visual spectacle that hints at the delicious surprises.

Baking the savory pastry twists is a transformative process that fills the kitchen with the irresistible aroma of butter and spicy goodness. The layers of dough puff up to golden perfection, creating a compelling contrast with the flavorful filling. Achieving the ideal crispness while maintaining a tender interior involves carefully balancing temperature and timing. As the twists emerge from the oven, their golden exteriors and enticing aromas beckon, setting the stage for a brunch experience that is both visually appealing and deliciously satisfying.

The versatility of savory pastry twists allows for myriad flavor combinations, making them a delightful addition to any Christmas brunch. Classic combinations such as ham and cheese or spinach and feta offer a timeless appeal, while more adventurous twists may feature ingredients like smoked salmon, caramelized onions, or sundried tomatoes. The art of flavor pairing becomes a creative expression, inviting bakers and cooks to experiment with ingredients that reflect the seasonal bounty and the preferences of the gathering.

Savory pastry twists also allow the incorporation of cultural influences and regional flavors into the Christmas brunch experience. A Mediterranean-inspired twist might showcase olives, feta, and sun-dried tomatoes, while an American Southwest twist could feature jalapeños, cheddar, and cilantro. The global appeal of savory pastry twists transcends culinary boundaries, offering a delightful journey for the taste buds that reflects the diversity of flavors and ingredients worldwide.

The visual appeal of savory pastry twists is a critical element of their allure, making them a treat for the palate and a feast for the eyes. The twisted and layered patterns, whether simple or intricate, create a sense of anticipation and celebration. Adding herbs, seeds, or a light brushing of egg wash enhances the golden sheen, adding to the overall aesthetic. The art of presentation elevates the humble pastry twist to a centerpiece that commands attention on the brunch table, inviting guests to indulge in a culinary experience that is as pleasing to the eye as it is to the taste buds.

The cultural and historical significance of savory pastries in holiday celebrations dates back centuries. In European traditions, delicious pastries have been a staple during festive seasons, offering a tangy counterpoint to the sweetness of holiday desserts. The British tradition of sausage rolls and the Scandinavian flair for spicy twists featuring smoked fish and dill exemplify how these treats have become integral to the tapestry of holiday feasting. As families and communities gather to celebrate Christmas, the presence of savory pastry twists becomes a link to culinary heritage and a nod to the timeless joy of communal dining.

Savoring savory pastry twists during Christmas brunch extends beyond the flavors and textures; it becomes a shared experience that fosters a sense of togetherness and conviviality. The communal act of tearing off a piece, revealing the layers within, adds an interactive element to the dining experience. The flavors of savory pastries catalyze conversation and connection as friends and family gather around the table to share in the festive abundance.

Savory pastry twists offer the added advantage of being versatile in preparation. They can be made and stored in the refrigerator or freezer, ready to be baked to perfection on brunch day. This convenience allows hosts to focus on enjoying the festivities and spending time with loved ones rather than being tied to the kitchen. The ease of preparation and impressive results make savory pastry twists an ideal addition to the holiday brunch repertoire.

Savory pastry twists embody the spirit of abundance and celebration in holiday entertainment. Their flaky layers, delicious fillings, and visual appeal create a feast for the senses, inviting guests to indulge in the joy of festive dining. Whether served as part of a Christmas brunch spread or as a delightful appetizer during holiday parties, savory pastry twists become a culinary expression of hospitality and shared enjoyment.

In conclusion, the art of crafting savory pastry twists for Christmas brunch is a celebration of flavors, textures, and visual allure. Each step involves a blend of precision and creativity, from the creation of the buttery pastry dough to the layering, filling, and baking process. As these delectable treats grace the holiday table, they become more than just pastries; they symbolize festive abundance, culinary craftsmanship, and the joy of shared moments with loved ones. Savory pastry twists, with their universal appeal and endless flavor possibilities, stand as a testament to the enduring magic of the culinary arts during the Christmas season and beyond.

CHAPTER VIII

The Art of Chocolate Making

Handmade Chocolate Truffles for Gifting

Handmade chocolate truffles, with their decadent richness and velvety textures, represent the epitome of indulgence and craftsmanship in the confectionery world. These exquisite treats, often reserved for special occasions, have transcended their humble origins to become symbols of refined taste and thoughtful gifting. Crafting chocolate truffles at home transforms a simple act of making sweets into a culinary art form, where the alchemy of chocolate and cream unfolds to create bite- sized masterpieces that delight the senses and evoke a sense of luxury.

At the heart of the chocolate truffle is the quality of its ingredients, with the choice of chocolate being paramount. Dark, milk, or white chocolate each lends its distinctive character to the truffle, setting the stage for a flavor journey ranging from intense and bittersweet to creamy and sweet. The art of selecting the right chocolate involves an understanding of cocoa percentages, flavor profiles, and the desired result. Whether using couverture chocolate or high-quality chocolate bars, the emphasis is on richness and depth, ensuring that each truffle is a harmonious marriage of cocoa and cream.

Making chocolate truffles begins with the ganache—a luscious mixture of melted chocolate and heated cream. The proportions of chocolate to cream and the temperature at which they are combined play a crucial role in achieving the desired texture. The velvety smoothness of the ganache results from the careful emulsion of these two ingredients, where the fat in the chocolate is evenly distributed within the liquid cream. This process requires patience and precision, as the emulsification sets the stage for the luxurious mouthfeel that defines a perfect chocolate truffle.

The flavor possibilities within chocolate truffles are as vast as the imagination allows. Classic truffle variations may incorporate natural extracts such as vanilla, coffee, or orange zest to enhance the chocolate's richness. For an adventurous twist, infusions of spices, herbs, or liquors like Grand Marnier, whiskey, or Chambord can elevate the truffles to new heights, adding complexity to the flavor profile. The art of flavoring chocolate truffles becomes a personalized expression of taste, allowing the maker to tailor each batch to suit their preferences or the recipient's palate.

Shaping and coating the ganache is the next step in the truffle-making process, transforming the velvety mixture into bite-sized confections. Traditionally, truffles are hand-rolled into small spheres, a tactile and intimate part of the craft that imparts a homemade charm. The rolling process requires a deft touch to achieve uniformity, and the hands-on approach allows for a connection between the maker and the creation. Alternatively, truffles can be piped into molds, producing uniform shapes that lend themselves to more intricate decorations and finishes.

The coating of chocolate truffles is an opportunity for artistic expression, providing a canvas for creativity and visual appeal. While the classic dusting of cocoa powder imparts an elegant simplicity, truffles can also be coated in melted chocolate, rolled in chopped nuts, or dipped in tempered chocolate for a glossy finish. Each coating option contributes to the aesthetics and the overall sensory experience, offering a delightful interplay of textures and flavors with each bite.

Handmade chocolate truffles are extraordinary in edible gifts, embodying the thoughtfulness and care of creating a present from scratch. Gifting homemade truffles transcends the commercial exchange of goods, becoming a gesture of personal connection and culinary artistry. Customizing flavors, shapes, and coatings allows the maker to tailor the truffles to the recipient's preferences, making the gift a unique and memorable experience.

The packaging of handmade chocolate truffles is the final touch that enhances their allure as gifts. Whether nestled in decorative boxes, adorned with ribbons, or placed in elegant tins, the presentation elevates the truffles to a level of sophistication that befits their decadent nature. The attention to detail in packaging extends the visual appeal of the truffles, turning them into a treat and a work of art that captures the essence of luxury and indulgence.

Beyond their role as gifts, handmade chocolate truffles have become popular at dessert tables, weddings, and special events. Their bite-sized nature makes them a versatile and crowd-pleasing addition to celebrations, offering a moment of indulgence that can be savored in a single bite. The aesthetic appeal of truffles, with their glossy finishes and creative coatings, adds a touch of elegance to any dessert spread, making them both a culinary delight and a visual centerpiece.

The culture of chocolate truffles has historical roots that trace back to the creative genius of a French chocolatier named Louis Dufour. In the late 19th century, Dufour is said to have accidentally poured hot cream over a bowl of chocolate chunks, creating a mixture that resembled the coveted black truffle fungus found in the Périgord region. The resulting confection, with its smooth ganache center and dusting of cocoa powder, became known as the chocolate truffle, forever altering the landscape of chocolate confections. Since then, chocolate truffles have evolved into a global phenomenon, with chocolatiers and home cooks exploring endless flavor combinations and artistic presentations.

The art of making chocolate truffles has evolved with advancements in chocolate production, allowing for a broader range of cocoa varieties and flavor profiles. The availability of high-quality chocolate couverture and the resurgence of artisanal chocolate makers have empowered truffle enthusiasts to experiment with single-origin chocolates, each with its unique terroir and tasting notes. This exploration of chocolate diversity adds a layer of sophistication to the craft, as makers can choose chocolates that highlight specific flavor nuances and complement the chosen infusions or coatings.

In recent years, the popularity of handmade chocolate truffles has been further fueled by the rise of craft chocolate and the emphasis on artisanal, small-batch production. Home cooks and professional chocolatiers alike have embraced the ethos of quality over quantity, elevating the art of chocolate-making to new heights. The use of ethically sourced and sustainably produced chocolate has become a priority for those who seek not only exquisite flavor but also an awareness of the environmental and social impact of their choices.

Making chocolate truffles at home has gained traction as a culinary pursuit that combines the joy of creating with the pleasure of savoring. From holiday gift-giving to intimate celebrations, crafting truffles becomes a labor of love that transcends the result. The tactile experience of working with chocolate, the aroma that fills the kitchen during melting and infusing, and the satisfaction of producing a batch of handmade confections contribute to the overall enjoyment of the craft.

In conclusion, handmade chocolate truffles stand as an epitome of confectionery artistry, combining the rich history of chocolate with the creativity of modern flavor profiles and presentations. From carefully selecting high-quality chocolate to the meticulous crafting of ganache, shaping, and coating, each step in the truffle-making process celebrates craftsmanship. Whether shared as gifts, featured on dessert tables, or enjoyed as personal indulgences, handmade chocolate truffles invite a moment of pure delight—a sensory experience that lingers on the palate and in the memory, leaving an enduring impression of luxury and culinary finesse.

Tempering Techniques for Stunning Chocolate Decorations

Tempering chocolate is a delicate and precise art transforming the humble cocoa bean into a glossy and snappy masterpiece. This culinary technique, born out of the desire to harness the full potential of chocolate's unique properties, is the key to achieving stunning chocolate decorations that captivate the eye and melt in the mouth with a satisfying snap. Tempering involves carefully manipulating the temperature of the chocolate to ensure the proper crystalline structure forms, allowing it to set with a smooth finish, glossy sheen, and a pleasing texture. The mastery of tempering techniques is a skill coveted by professional chocolatiers and an accessible and rewarding pursuit for home cooks and aspiring chocolate enthusiasts.

Tempering chocolate begins with selecting high-quality chocolate couverture, which typically contains more cocoa butter than compound chocolates. Cocoa butter, the natural fat in cocoa beans, gives chocolate its luxurious mouthfeel and the ability to form stable crystals during tempering. Couverture chocolate provides the ideal canvas for creating decorations due to its superior quality and the presence of cocoa butter, which contributes to the desired characteristics of tempered chocolate.

There are several methods of tempering chocolate, each requiring a keen understanding of temperature control and precise techniques. One of the traditional methods is the seeding technique, where chocolate is melted gently until it reaches a specific temperature, cooled down by adding small pieces of unmelted chocolate (seeds), and then gently reheated. This process encourages the formation of stable crystals in the chocolate, ensuring a smooth and glossy finish. The seeding method is favored for its simplicity and reliability, making it a go-to technique for professionals and home bakers.

Another popular tempering method is the tabling technique, which involves spreading melted chocolate thinly on an excellent surface, agitating it to encourage crystal formation, and then bringing it back into the melted chocolate. This technique requires finesse and experience, as the chocolate needs to be worked quickly and efficiently on a calm surface to achieve the desired temper. The tabling method is known for producing chocolate with a crisp snap and a high gloss, making it a preferred technique for creating intricate decorations.

A more modern approach to tempering involves using a chocolate tempering machine, which automates the tempering process. These machines control the temperature of the chocolate at each stage, ensuring precision and consistency. While tempering machines are a convenient option for large-scale production in professional kitchens, they also offer a user-friendly experience for home cooks looking to achieve perfect tempering without the complexity of manual techniques. The ease of use and efficiency make tempering machines attractive for those seeking a streamlined chocolate tempering process.

Regardless of the method chosen, the tempering process involves three key temperature stages: melting, cooling, and reheating. The chocolate is initially melted to a temperature that fully liquifies it, breaking down any existing crystals. It is then cooled down to a specific temperature, allowing the stable crystals to form. Finally, the chocolate is gently reheated to a working temperature that maintains its fluidity while preserving the desired crystalline structure. The careful control of temperatures at each stage is crucial to achieving the perfect temper and the desired characteristics in the finished chocolate.

The effect of tempering on chocolate's physical properties is evident in the result. Well-tempered chocolate will have a glossy appearance, a smooth texture, and a satisfying snap when broken. The absence of streaks or dull patches indicates a successful temper, as does the pleasant mouthfeel from the proper alignment of cocoa butter crystals. The importance of achieving the correct temper cannot be overstated, as it enhances the visual appeal of chocolate decorations and contributes to the overall sensory experience.

The art of tempering extends beyond the basic techniques to include the creation of intricate chocolate decorations that add a touch of elegance to desserts and confections. From delicate curls and swirls to elaborate sculptures and molds, tempered chocolate becomes a versatile medium for artistic expression. The controlled fluidity of tempered chocolate allows for precise piping and drizzling, making it ideal for creating fine lines, delicate shapes, and intricate designs that elevate the aesthetic of desserts.

Chocolate curls, a classic and visually stunning decoration, are created by thinning tempered chocolate on an excellent surface, allowing it to set partially, and then using a scraper or knife to create curls as the chocolate is lifted. These curls can be arranged on cakes, tarts, or desserts, adding a touch of sophistication and a burst of chocolate flavor. The process requires a steady hand and some practice, but the results are well worth the effort.

Swirls and drizzles are another effective way to incorporate tempered chocolate into dessert presentations. Using a piping bag or a spoon, the tempered chocolate can be swirled or drizzled over desserts, creating eye-catching patterns and adding a layer of flavor and texture. This technique is prevalent in decorating individual pastries, cupcakes, or even a simple bowl of ice cream, turning an essential treat into a visually appealing and indulgent experience.

Tempered chocolate can be molded and sculpted into intricate shapes and figures for those with a more artistic inclination. From delicate chocolate flowers to elaborate sculptures, the possibilities are limited only by imagination and skill. The malleability of tempered chocolate, when at the correct temperature, allows for the creation of three-dimensional decorations that add a show-stopping element to desserts and displays.

Beyond its aesthetic appeal, tempered chocolate also serves a functional confectionery function. It acts as a protective shell for fillings in bonbons and truffles, preventing them from oozing or leaking. The snap of tempered chocolate contrasts the creaminess of fillings, creating a harmonious balance of textures in each bite. Combining tempered and flavorful fillings is a hallmark of fine chocolate craftsmanship.

Tempering techniques are not limited to dark chocolate; they are equally applicable to milk and white chocolates. Each type of chocolate requires specific attention to temperature ranges due to variations in cocoa content and sugar levels. While dark chocolate generally has a higher cocoa content and a more pronounced flavor profile, milk chocolate contains added dairy ingredients for a creamier taste, and white chocolate relies on cocoa butter for its richness without cocoa solids. The ability to temper different types of chocolate expands the possibilities for creating diverse and visually stunning decorations that cater to various tastes.

The mastery of tempering techniques has its challenges, and even experienced chocolatiers may encounter variations in temper due to factors such as ambient temperature, humidity, or the specific characteristics of different chocolate batches. However, pursuing perfect tempering becomes a journey of continuous learning and refinement, where each attempt brings insights into the intricacies of the chocolate tempering process. The hands-on experience of working with chocolate, understanding its behavior, and developing an intuitive sense of temperatures contribute to honing tempering skills over time.

In conclusion, the art of tempering chocolate is a transformative process that elevates this beloved confection into a medium for artistic expression. From the controlled crystallization of cocoa butter to the creation of intricate decorations, tempering techniques play a pivotal role in chocolate craftsmanship. The glossy finish, smooth texture, and satisfying snap of tempered chocolate enhance the visual appeal of desserts and contribute to the overall sensory experience. Whether crafting delicate curls, intricate swirls, or elaborate sculptures, the mastery of tempering techniques empowers chocolatiers and home cooks alike to create stunning chocolate decorations that are as pleasing to the eye as they are to the palate. In chocolate confections, tempering is the alchemy that transforms a simple ingredient into an edible work of art.

CHAPTER IX

Edible Gifts from the Heart

Personalized Treats for Homemade Gift Baskets

Creating personalized treats for homemade gift baskets is a heartfelt and meaningful way to share joy and express thoughtfulness. The art of curating a collection of handmade delights allows individuals to infuse their personality and care into each component, turning a simple assortment of treats into a cherished gift. Whether for holidays, birthdays, or special occasions, crafting personalized treats adds a touch of sincerity that resonates with the recipient. From delectable cookies and candies to artisanal jams and preserves, each item in the gift basket becomes a testament to the time, effort, and creativity invested in creating a truly unique and memorable present.

At the heart of personalized treat gift baskets is the intention to tailor the selection to the tastes and preferences of the recipient. This bespoke approach requires understanding the recipient's favorite flavors, dietary restrictions, and culinary inclinations. Armed with this knowledge, the gift giver can curate a collection of treats that not only delights the palate but also communicates a sense of thoughtfulness and consideration. The personalized touch transforms the gift from a generic offering into a reflection of the recipient's individuality.

Cookies, often considered the quintessential homemade treat, offer many possibilities for personalization. From classic chocolate chip cookies to exotic flavor combinations like lavender-infused shortbread or chai-spiced snickerdoodles, the options are limited only by the baker's imagination. Personalized cookies can be shaped into initials, favorite animals, or themed designs that resonate with the recipient's interests. Packaging these cookies in decorative boxes or jars adds an extra layer of charm, turning them into a sweet treat and a visual delight.

Candies, whether handcrafted caramels, flavored truffles, or custom lollipops, provide another avenue for personalization. Experimenting with unique flavor infusions, such as sea salt, rosemary caramels, or champagne-infused truffles, allows the creator to showcase their culinary ingenuity. The artful presentation of candies in vibrant wrappers, decorative tins, or clear cellophane bags with ribbons enhances the visual appeal, inviting the recipient to indulge in a sweet symphony of flavors.

Artisanal jams, preserves, and spreads offer a delightful way to incorporate homemade goodness into gift baskets. Creating personalized flavors, such as strawberry balsamic jam or spiced apple butter, adds a unique twist to the classic preserves. Pairing these spreads with freshly baked bread or artisan crackers creates a complete and thoughtful tasting experience. The jars, adorned with charming labels or fabric covers, contribute to the overall aesthetics of the gift basket, making it a visual treat as well.

Infusing a bit of homemade warmth into the gift basket can extend beyond baked goods to include savory treats. Custom spice blends, seasoned nuts, or flavored oils showcase the creator's culinary prowess and offer a piquant counterpart to the sweet offerings. Personalized popcorn mixes, seasoned with unique blends of herbs and spices, add a gourmet touch and create a delightful balance within the gift basket.

The art of personalization can also extend to beverages, with homemade drink mixes or infused syrups becoming delightful additions. Crafting custom hot chocolate or chai blends allows the gift giver to cater to the recipient's taste preferences, whether they enjoy a hint of peppermint, a dash of cinnamon, or the richness of dark chocolate. Infused syrups for coffee or cocktails, such as vanilla bean or lavender-infused simple syrup, provide a versatile and flavorful element to the gift basket.

Packaging personalized treats is a crucial aspect of creating a visually appealing and cohesive gift basket. Thoughtfully chosen containers, such as decorative boxes, mason jars, or woven baskets, serve as the canvas for arranging and presenting the treats. Personalized labels, tags, or handwritten notes add a charming touch, conveying a sense of care and consideration. The arrangement of treats within the basket can be an art form, with layering, height variations, and color coordination contributing to the overall aesthetics.

Creating personalized treat gift baskets goes beyond the tangible items; it involves infusing the gift with emotion and sentiment. Handwritten recipe cards, sharing the origin or inspiration behind each treat, add a personal and intimate element. Including a heartfelt note or a customized message expressing well wishes and affection elevates the gift to a meaningful gesture beyond mere consumption.

The beauty of personalized treat gift baskets lies in their versatility and adaptability to various occasions. Seasonal treats such as gingerbread cookies, peppermint bark, or spiced nuts can evoke a festive spirit for holidays. Birthdays offer an opportunity to tailor the treats to the recipient's favorite flavors or indulge in decadent desserts like personalized birthday cakes in a jar. Celebratory occasions can be marked with champagne-infused truffles or gourmet popcorn mixes. The ability to customize the treats based on the occasion makes personalized gift baskets a versatile and thoughtful gift-giving option.

Beyond the joy of receiving, creating personalized treat gift baskets is a fulfilling and creative endeavor. It allows the gift giver to channel their passion for baking, cooking, or crafting into a tangible expression of care.

Experimenting with flavors, testing recipes, and selecting the perfect packaging becomes a labor of love that is both therapeutic and rewarding. Gifting extends the creator's personality, connecting the giver and the recipient.

In a world where commercialization often dominates the gift-giving landscape, personalized treat gift baskets are a testament to the enduring value of handmade and thoughtful presents. They transcend the transactional nature of store-bought gifts, embodying the essence of generosity and personal connection. Whether exchanged between friends, family members, or colleagues, these personalized treats become symbols of appreciation, gratitude, and the simple joy of sharing homemade goodness.

In conclusion, the art of creating personalized treat gift baskets celebrates creativity, thoughtfulness, and the joy of sharing homemade delights. From carefully curated selections of cookies and candies to artisanal jams, spreads, and savory treats, each element contributes to a unique and heartfelt gift. The act of personalization extends beyond flavors to include the presentation, packaging, and the emotional connection forged between the giver and the recipient. In a world where meaningful gestures often stand out, personalized treat gift baskets shine as a beacon of sincerity, encapsulating the warmth and generosity that defines the spirit of gift-giving.

Packaging and Presentation Ideas

Packaging and presentation are integral aspects of the culinary world, transforming homemade treats and gourmet delights into visual masterpieces that captivate the senses. The art of packaging extends beyond mere functionality; it is a creative expression that enhances the overall experience of receiving and enjoying delectable offerings. From the simple elegance of classic packaging to the avant-garde allure of innovative presentations, the packaging of culinary delights plays a pivotal role in shaping perceptions, evoking emotions, and elevating the appreciation of the culinary craft.

One classic packaging approach involves using traditional materials and designs that exude timeless elegance. Brown kraft paper, adorned with twine or ribbon, imparts a rustic charm to cookies, candies, and artisanal treats. This classic packaging adds a touch of nostalgia and communicates a sense of simplicity and authenticity. Using wax paper or parchment inside the packaging helps maintain freshness and prevents treats from sticking, ensuring that the visual appeal aligns with the quality of the contents.

In the realm of cookies and baked goods, the iconic cookie tin has been a staple in packaging for generations. Whether adorned with festive designs for the holidays or showcasing vintage patterns, cookie tins provide a versatile and reusable packaging option. The variety in shapes and sizes allows for customization, while the sturdy construction protects delicate treats during transport. The nostalgia associated with opening a cookie tin and discovering an array of homemade delights adds a layer of joy to the gift-giving experience.

For a touch of sophistication, clear cellophane bags or boxes showcase the treats within, allowing their colors and textures to shine through. This transparent packaging is particularly effective for visually appealing treats such as candies, macarons, or chocolate-covered strawberries. Tied with a satin ribbon or sealed with a custom sticker, clear packaging exudes a modern and elegant aesthetic, making it a popular choice for wedding favors, upscale events, and gourmet gifts.

Custom labels and tags add a personalized and professional touch to packaged treats. Whether handwritten with a personal message, printed with a decorative design, or featuring the creator's logo, labels contribute to the overall branding and presentation. They serve not only as identifiers but also as visual elements that enhance the aesthetic appeal of the packaging.

Coordinating the colors and styles of labels with the overall theme creates a cohesive and polished look, turning simple packaging into a curated experience.

In the realm of confections, the art of packaging extends to the design of candy boxes and chocolate packaging. Delicate truffles, pralines, or handmade chocolates often find their home in intricately designed boxes, each compartment cradling a unique flavor or filling. Embossed or foil-stamped logos on chocolate boxes add a touch of luxury, elevating the perception of the treats within. Custom-shaped chocolate boxes, mimicking the form of cacao pods or elegant geometric patterns, showcase the craftsmanship and creativity involved in the chocolate-making process.

Jar packaging has become a popular and versatile option for presenting an array of treats, from jams and preserves to layered cookie mixes. With their nostalgic charm, Mason jars evoke a sense of homeliness and simplicity. Layering ingredients in a visually appealing manner within the jar not only adds an artistic touch but also allows the recipient to see the components of the treat. Tied with a fabric square or adorned with a custom tag, jarred treats become charming gifts suitable for various occasions.

For the holiday season, festive packaging takes center stage, with themed designs and colors adding a joyful touch to treats. Red and green hues, snowflakes, and holly motifs convey a sense of celebration and merriment. Tin tie bags, adorned with holiday-themed illustrations or prints, are a convenient and festive option for packaging cookies, candies, and small treats. The use of seasonal elements in packaging enhances the overall experience, making the treats delicious and visually resonant with the holiday spirit.

Beyond the traditional, unconventional materials and creative presentations offer a fresh perspective on packaging. Wooden crates or baskets lined with decorative paper or fabric create a charming, rustic display for various treats. This approach is efficient for larger gift baskets, showcasing a variety of items such as baked goods, jams, and savory treats. The juxtaposition of natural materials with vibrant colors and textures adds an eclectic and artisanal flair to the overall presentation.

In the modern era, eco-friendly packaging has gained prominence, aligning with a growing awareness of sustainable practices. Recyclable and biodegradable materials like cardboard, paper, and glass are preferred for environmentally conscious packaging. Minimalist designs, emphasizing natural textures and subdued colors, reflect a commitment to sustainability while maintaining an aesthetic appeal. Bamboo or wooden packaging elements further contribute to the eco-friendly theme, creating a harmonious balance between aesthetics and environmental responsibility.

The concept of edible packaging takes the presentation of treats to a new level, blurring the lines between the container and its contents. For example, cookies or pastries can be placed in edible boxes made from chocolate or cookie dough. The delightful surprise of enjoying the treats inside and the packaging itself adds a playful and innovative dimension to the gift-giving experience. This approach is prevalent for special occasions and events where surprise and novelty enhance overall enjoyment.

Personalization in packaging goes beyond the visual to include scents and aromas. Infusing packaging materials with the fragrance of herbs, spices, or essential oils adds a multisensory dimension to the presentation. For example, lavender-scented packaging enhances the experience of receiving a gift of lavender-infused cookies or sachets. This thoughtful touch engages the olfactory senses, creating a more immersive and memorable experience for the recipient.

The size and shape of packaging can also be tailored to suit the specific nature of the treats. Miniature boxes or bags are ideal for individual cookies, truffles, or petite confections. Larger boxes or tins accommodate an assortment of treats, providing a diverse and indulgent experience. Custom-shaped packaging, molded to resemble the treats inside or themed to match the occasion, adds an element of whimsy and surprise.

In the digital age, the art of packaging extends to the virtual realm with the rise of e-gifting and online deliveries. Virtual gift cards, digital illustrations, and personalized messages contribute to the online presentation of culinary delights. The anticipation and excitement generated through creative digital presentations enhance the overall experience of receiving and enjoying treats, even from a distance.

Packaging and presenting culinary delights is an art that transcends the functional aspects of containment. It is a creative endeavor that involves storytelling, aesthetics, and a deep understanding of the recipient's preferences. The choice of materials, colors, and designs communicates a message, whether it's one of elegance, warmth, playfulness, or sustainability. Thoughtful packaging elevates the act of giving and receiving, turning a simple exchange of treats into a visual and sensory journey.

In conclusion, packaging and presentation are integral to the culinary experience, shaping perceptions and enhancing the enjoyment of treats. From classic elegance to avant-garde innovation, packaging encompasses a wide range of styles and materials. Whether through traditional cookie tins, transparent cellophane bags, or eco-friendly options, each choice adds a layer of meaning to the act of giving and receiving culinary delights. The evolution of packaging reflects not only changing trends and preferences but also a commitment to sustainability, creativity, and a multisensory approach that engages the recipient on various levels. In a world where visual appeal and experiential elements play a significant role, packaging becomes a powerful tool for expressing creativity, thoughtfulness, and the joy of sharing delightful treats.

CHAPTER X

Creating a Magical Christmas Baking Atmosphere

Setting the Mood with Festive Music and Décor

Setting the mood with festive music and décor is an art form that transcends the visual and auditory senses, creating an immersive experience that captures the spirit of celebration and joy. Whether hosting a holiday gathering, a festive dinner party, or simply infusing the home with seasonal cheer, the combination of carefully selected music and thoughtfully curated décor transforms the atmosphere, evoking memories, emotions, and a sense of togetherness.

With its unique ability to evoke emotions and stir nostalgia, music plays a central role in setting the festive mood. The sounds of jingling bells, cheerful melodies, and timeless classics instantly transport individuals to the heart of the holiday season. With their rich history and universal appeal, traditional carols serve as the quintessential soundtrack for festive gatherings. Whether it's the joyous notes of "Jingle Bells," the soulful rendition of "Silent Night," or the upbeat tempo of "Deck the Halls," each carol contributes to a musical tapestry that resonates with the essence of the holidays.

Beyond the classics, contemporary holiday music adds a vibrant modern touch to the festive ambiance. Artists across genres infuse their unique styles into seasonal tunes, offering a diverse selection that caters to various tastes. From pop renditions of familiar carols to original compositions that capture the contemporary spirit of the season, modern holiday music complements the traditional, creating a dynamic and engaging playlist.

Curating a festive music playlist involves a thoughtful blend of familiar favorites and discoveries. The playlist serves as a backdrop, enhancing the mood without overpowering conversations or activities. Instrumental arrangements of holiday classics provide a soothing and elegant option for background music, creating a warm and inviting atmosphere. Including instrumental ensembles, such as orchestras or jazz bands, adds a touch of sophistication to the auditory experience, making it suitable for formal gatherings and cozy family celebrations.

In the age of streaming services, the accessibility of holiday music is unparalleled. Platforms like Spotify, Apple Music, and Pandora offer curated playlists spanning various styles and moods. This convenience allows hosts and enthusiasts to explore diverse genres, discover new interpretations of familiar tunes, and tailor the musical ambiance to suit the occasion. The collaborative nature of playlist creation also enables friends and family to contribute their favorite holiday songs, fostering a shared ownership in shaping the festive soundtrack.

The synchronization of music with décor creates a cohesive and immersive experience, engaging multiple senses to amplify the festive atmosphere. Décor serves as the visual expression of the holiday spirit, weaving together colors, textures, and thematic elements to convey a sense of warmth and celebration. The traditional color palette of red, green, and gold, enriched by accents of silver or white, forms the basis for classic holiday décor. This timeless combination evokes a sense of tradition and nostalgia, providing a visual link to cherished memories of holidays past.

The iconic image of evergreen foliage, adorned with twinkling lights and ornaments, remains a symbol of holiday décor. Whether natural or artificial, Christmas trees serve as the focal point of many festive settings.

Decorating the tree, a cherished tradition involves placing ornaments that hold sentimental value—stringing lights that cast a warm glow. I am crowning with a star or angel. The visual impact of a well-decorated tree extends beyond aesthetics; it becomes a tangible representation of the holiday spirit, radiating joy and nostalgia.

Wreaths, garlands, and swags crafted from evergreen branches or artificial materials extend the theme of greenery throughout the home. Adorned with ribbons, bows, and festive embellishments, these decorative elements add a touch of nature and elegance to walls, doors, and mantels. The fragrance of fresh evergreen, whether from a wreath or a centerpiece, further enhances the sensory experience, infusing the air with the unmistakable scent of the season.

With their magical glow, lights play a transformative role in holiday décor. Strings of fairy lights wrapped around banisters, draped across mantels, or hung on walls create a whimsical and enchanting ambiance. The warm and inviting glow of candlelight, whether from traditional candles or electric alternatives, adds a touch of intimacy and coziness to the setting. Adorned with festive motifs or reflective surfaces, candle holders amplify the luminous effect, casting a soft and flattering light on the surroundings.

Ornaments, ranging from delicate glass baubles to whimsical figurines, contribute to the personalization of holiday décor. Each ornament carries a story, whether it's a handmade creation, a cherished heirloom, or a representation of a significant memory. The act of hanging ornaments becomes a ritual, with each piece adding to the overall narrative of the festive season. Themed ornament collections, such as a set depicting winter woodland creatures or a series of vintage-inspired designs, provide the tree with a cohesive and curated look.

Table settings become a canvas for expressing the holiday theme through décor. Festive tablecloths, napkins, and placemats adorned with seasonal patterns or motifs set the stage for memorable gatherings. Crafted from a combination of candles, greenery, and decorative elements, centerpieces become focal points that draw attention and spark conversation. The use of thematic dishware, whether featuring traditional holiday scenes or contemporary designs, adds an extra layer of visual interest to the dining experience.

Inflatable decorations and lawn displays contribute to extending festive ambiance beyond indoor spaces. Larger-than-life Santa Clauses, snowmen, and twinkling lights in outdoor settings create a sense of community and shared celebration. The act of outdoor decoration becomes a collective endeavor, with neighborhoods illuminated by the glow of festive displays. The visual impact of well-coordinated outdoor décor fosters a sense of camaraderie and amplifies the overall holiday spirit.

Themed décor allows individuals to tailor the visual elements to specific holiday traditions or cultural influences. Whether embracing a winter wonderland theme with snowflakes and icicles or incorporating cultural symbols and colors, the choice of décor becomes a personal expression of the individual or family's connection to the holiday season. Hanukkah celebrations may feature blue and white color schemes, with menorahs and dreidels as prominent elements. Kwanzaa décor may incorporate the symbolic colors of red, green, and black, along with traditional symbols like the kinara and unity cup.

The concept of a holiday village or diorama adds a whimsical and storytelling dimension to décor. Miniature houses, figurines, and scenes create a charming tableau that captures the imagination and invites viewers to explore the festive landscape. These small displays can be thematic, with scenes representing a winter village, a bustling holiday market, or even a North Pole workshop. The interactive and narrative aspect of such displays engages both adults and children, fostering a sense of wonder and delight.

Personalized and handmade décor elements create a unique and meaningful environment. Handcrafted ornaments, DIY wreaths, and homemade garlands add a personal touch that transcends mass-produced decorations. Incorporating family traditions, such as handmade stockings or personalized ornaments with names and dates, creates a sense of continuity and shared history. Crafting décor becomes a cherished activity, fostering a sense of connection and creativity.

In contemporary design, minimalist and modern approaches to holiday décor offer a fresh and stylish aesthetic. Simplified color palettes, unconventional materials, and sleek designs create a striking, sophisticated look. White and metallic tones, geometric shapes, and clean lines evoke a modern winter wonderland. Alternative tree designs, such as wall decals, ladder displays, or sculptural interpretations, challenge traditional notions of holiday décor, appealing to those with a more contemporary sensibility.

The integration of technology into holiday décor introduces interactive and dynamic elements. Intelligent lighting systems, programmable decorations, and projection mapping enable individuals to create ever-changing displays. The synchronization of lights with music, whether through traditional methods or smart home technology, adds a dynamic and entertaining aspect to the festive environment. The marriage of technology and décor opens new possibilities for creative expression and customization.

In conclusion, setting the mood with festive music and décor is a multifaceted and creative endeavor that engages the senses and evokes the spirit of celebration. Combining carefully curated music playlists and thoughtfully arranged décor creates an immersive experience that transcends the visual and auditory realms. Whether through the timeless sounds of traditional carols or contemporary artists' modern interpretations, music is a powerful tool for creating atmosphere and fostering a sense of togetherness.

Concurrently, décor transforms spaces into festive landscapes, utilizing colors, textures, and thematic elements to convey warmth and holiday cheer. From the iconic imagery of Christmas trees and wreaths to the personalization of handmade ornaments and modern design aesthetics, holiday décor becomes a canvas for storytelling and self-expression. Festive music and décor form a harmonious symphony that resonates with the holiday season's joy, nostalgia, and shared traditions.

Baking with Family and Friends: A Joyous Tradition

Baking transcends the mere act of preparing food; it transforms into a vessel of cherished memories, a conduit for bonding, and a repository of tradition when shared with family and friends. This timeless practice has been woven into the fabric of cultures worldwide, serving as a universal thread that connects generations and fosters a sense of togetherness. With its aromatic symphony of ingredients, the kitchen becomes a haven where the joy of creation mingles with the warmth of companionship. This section explores the significance of baking as a communal activity, delving into how it strengthens familial and friendly ties, imparts valuable life lessons, and preserves the intangible but enduring essence of shared experiences.

When embarking on a baking adventure with loved ones, the kitchen becomes a dynamic canvas where individuals of varying ages, skills, and backgrounds converge. The rhythmic hum of the mixer, the tantalizing aroma of ingredients melding together, and the shared anticipation of the final outcome create a sensory experience that transcends the culinary domain. Family and friends exchange stories, laughter, and advice in this communal space, weaving an intricate tapestry of shared memories. Once just a utilitarian space, the kitchen transforms into a hub of connection, where generations connect over a shared love for creating something delicious.

One of the critical facets of baking with family and friends lies in the collaborative nature of the activity. Each person, whether a seasoned baker or a novice, brings unique skills and perspectives to the kitchen. Grandparents may impart age-old family recipes, while children infuse the atmosphere with unbridled enthusiasm. This intergenerational exchange fosters a sense of continuity, linking the past with the present and ensuring that culinary traditions endure. Passing down recipes becomes a sacred rite, preserving the ingredients and techniques and the stories and sentiments attached to them.

Furthermore, the collaborative spirit inherent in baking imparts valuable life lessons to those involved. Patience, teamwork, and the art of compromise emerge as family members and friends work together to create something delightful. While measuring ingredients and waiting for the oven timer to chime, individuals learn the importance of perseverance and the rewards of a collective effort. Baking becomes a microcosm of life itself, a metaphor for the intricate dance of collaboration and individual contribution.

Beyond the immediate joys of the baking process, the shared experience of creating something from scratch cultivates a sense of accomplishment and pride. As the fruits of labor emerge from the oven, golden and fragrant, a collective satisfaction envelops the kitchen. This shared achievement reinforces the bonds between participants, creating a shared legacy that extends beyond the confines of the kitchen. Baking becomes a source of family and friendship pride, with each creation serving as a tangible testament to the love and effort invested by all.

In addition to fostering connections, baking with family and friends provides a unique platform for cultural exchange. The kitchen becomes a melting pot where diverse traditions converge, allowing individuals to explore and appreciate the rich tapestry of global culinary heritage. Whether exchanging traditional recipes, experimenting with exotic ingredients, or infusing a familiar dish with a novel twist, baking celebrates diversity. This cultural exchange broadens culinary horizons and fosters an environment of openness and acceptance among participants.

The tradition of baking with loved ones also acts as a powerful antidote to the frenetic pace of modern life. In a world characterized by constant connectivity and rapid technological advancements, gathering in the kitchen becomes a sanctuary of presence and mindfulness. The tactile nature of baking, from measuring ingredients to kneading dough, grounds individuals in the present moment. It offers a respite from the outside world's demands, creating a shared space where family and friends can be fully present with one another.

Moreover, baking with loved ones is a bulwark against the erosion of familial bonds in an era marked by busy schedules and digital distractions. In the shared pursuit of a common goal, whether a decadent cake or a batch of cookies, individuals find solace in the familiarity of familial and friendly ties. The kitchen, therefore, becomes a refuge where the ebb and flow of life can be momentarily set aside, allowing for genuine connections to flourish. In a society where the definition of family is evolving, baking together reaffirms the enduring importance of shared experiences.

As with any tradition, baking with family and friends evolves, adapting to changing circumstances and societal dynamics. In the face of challenges, the kitchen becomes a resilient space where individuals can find solace and strength in shared rituals. Whether celebrating milestones, navigating difficult times, or simply coming together for the joy of creation, baking is a constant, a reassuring anchor that weathers the storms of life.

In conclusion, baking with family and friends is a joyous tradition that transcends the boundaries of culinary practice. It is a timeless endeavor that weaves together the threads of connection, collaboration, and cultural exchange. Through the shared experience of creating something delicious, individuals strengthen familial and friendly ties and impart valuable life lessons to one another. Baking becomes a repository of cherished memories, a sanctuary of presence, and a resilient tradition that endures through the ebb and flow of life. In the warm embrace of the kitchen, surrounded by the laughter and love of those we hold dear, baking becomes a celebration of the enduring bonds that define our shared human experience.

CHAPTER XI

Troubleshooting and Tips

Common Christmas Baking Challenges and Solutions

The festive season is synonymous with the warm aroma of spices, the sweet melody of holiday tunes, and the joyous hustle and bustle of preparing special treats. Christmas baking, a beloved tradition for many, transforms kitchens into bustling workshops where families and friends gather to create delectable delights. Yet, amidst the merriment, even the most seasoned bakers may encounter challenges that threaten to dampen the holiday spirit. In this section, we explore common Christmas baking challenges and offer practical solutions, ensuring that the season remains a time of joy, celebration, and the sweet satisfaction of successfully overcoming culinary hurdles.

One of the perennial challenges bakers face during the holiday season is achieving the perfect moisture balance in baked goods. Whether it's cookies, cakes, or bread, the winter air can be arid, leading to crumbly textures and overly dry treats. The solution lies in meticulous ingredient measurements and thoughtful adjustments. Increasing the moisture content with ingredients such as applesauce, yogurt, or sour cream can rescue a dry batter, ensuring a final product that is moist and flavorful. Additionally, covering baked goods with a damp cloth while cooling or storing them in airtight containers helps retain moisture and keeps treats fresh for extended periods.

Another hurdle that often arises in Christmas baking is the dreaded issue of cookies spreading too much or not enough. Achieving the perfect cookie – golden on the edges with a chewy or crispy center – requires careful consideration of ingredients and temperature. To combat excessive spreading, chilling the cookie dough before baking helps solidify the fats, preventing cookies from flattening too quickly. Conversely, if cookies are too thick, a higher baking temperature for a shorter duration can promote spreading while maintaining a soft interior. This delicate dance between ingredients and oven temperature ensures that each batch of Christmas cookies emerges from the oven with the desired texture and appearance.

The quest for the ideal texture extends beyond cookies to encompass the realm of cakes, where achieving a light and fluffy crumb can be elusive. Overmixing the batter, a common pitfall, can lead to a dense and tough cake. The remedy lies in a gentle hand and incorporating ingredients just until they are combined. Additionally, sifting dry ingredients before adding them to the wet mixture prevents clumps, contributing to a smoother batter and a more uniform texture. Patience during the mixing process is key – the goal is not speed but rather the careful amalgamation of ingredients to create a tender and ethereally light cake.

For those venturing into the world of yeast-based Christmas treats, such as cinnamon rolls or stollen, achieving the perfect rise can be daunting. Yeast, a living organism, requires the right environment to flourish; factors like temperature and freshness play crucial roles. Ensuring that yeast is not expired and activating it in warm (but not hot) liquid provides the ideal conditions for fermentation. Placing the dough in a draft-free area to rise, covered with a damp cloth, allows the yeast to work its magic, resulting in a beautifully risen and flavorful Christmas masterpiece.

The festive season often beckons bakers to experiment with intricate designs and shapes, from gingerbread houses to intricately decorated sugar cookies. However, maintaining the structural integrity of these creations can be a source of frustration. Gingerbread houses may collapse, and delicate cookie shapes may lose their definition during baking. The key lies in selecting a sturdy gingerbread recipe that includes the right balance of ingredients, ensuring a firm yet flavorful structure. For intricate cookie shapes, freezing the dough before baking helps maintain their form during the oven's heat. Additionally, allowing baked goods to cool completely before attempting any decorative elements ensures that icing and embellishments adhere securely, creating stunning and structurally sound edible works of art.

Even the most meticulous bakers can encounter the issue of desserts sticking to pans or molds, turning what should be a joyous occasion into a frustrating ordeal. The solution lies in proper preparation and the strategic use of ingredients. Greasing pans with a generous layer of butter or using parchment paper prevents sticking and facilitates easy removal. Dusting with flour or cocoa powder can enhance the release process for intricate molds. Patience is crucial during the unmolding stage – allowing baked goods to cool slightly before attempting to release them ensures that they maintain their shape and appearance.

Despite careful planning and precise measurements, ovens can sometimes throw a curveball by cooking unevenly, leading to unevenly browned or undercooked portions of baked goods. This challenge can be addressed by understanding the peculiarities of the oven and making simple adjustments. Rotating baking sheets or pans halfway through the baking time ensures that each portion receives an equal share of heat. Investing in an oven thermometer provides an accurate temperature gauge, allowing bakers to compensate for any variations in their oven's performance. By becoming attuned to the nuances of their baking environment, individuals can master the art of even baking, ensuring consistent results with each batch.

The pursuit of picture-perfect treats often leads bakers to experiment with food coloring and decorative elements. However, achieving vibrant hues without altering the texture or flavor of the final product can be challenging.

Natural ingredients, such as fruit purees or vegetable juices, offer a solution by infusing color without the need for artificial additives. Careful experimentation with the quantity of natural coloring agents allows bakers to achieve the desired shades while maintaining the recipe's integrity. This approach not only enhances the visual appeal of Christmas treats but also aligns with a growing preference for natural and wholesome ingredients.

In the realm of holiday baking, the challenge of time management can cast a shadow over the joyous process. With multiple recipes to tackle, each with its unique steps and timings, orchestrating a seamless production line requires careful planning. The solution lies in creating a detailed schedule that accounts for preparation, baking, and cooling times for each recipe. Prioritizing tasks based on their complexity and interweaving more straightforward steps with more involved ones allows bakers to maximize efficiency. Additionally, enlisting the help of family or friends can transform the baking process into a collaborative and enjoyable undertaking, turning the challenge of time management into an opportunity for shared memories.

In conclusion, the art of Christmas baking, while imbued with joy and tradition, has its challenges. From achieving the perfect texture to managing time effectively, bakers navigate a complex landscape of potential pitfalls. However, with a combination of knowledge, creativity, and a dash of holiday spirit, these challenges can be transformed into opportunities for growth and learning. The solutions offered here provide a guide for bakers to overcome common obstacles, ensuring that the festive season remains a time of culinary delight shared with loved ones. As ovens warm and kitchens fill with the tantalizing scents of holiday spices, the challenges of Christmas baking become stepping stones on creating cherished memories and delectable treats that will be savored for years to come.

Expert Tips for Perfect Holiday Treats

The holiday season brings a palpable sense of joy and anticipation, often centered around the creation and indulgence of delectable treats. Whether it's the rich aroma of gingerbread wafting through the kitchen or the sight of a perfectly adorned yule log, holiday treats can evoke cherished memories and create a festive atmosphere. To elevate your culinary endeavors during this particular time, expert tips can serve as invaluable guides, ensuring that your creations are not only delicious but also a source of pride. In this section, we delve into a treasure trove of wisdom from seasoned bakers and culinary experts, offering insights into the art of crafting perfect holiday treats.

One of the foundational principles experts emphasize is the importance of precise measurements. Baking, more than any other culinary pursuit, is a science where exact proportions are critical to success. Renowned pastry chefs and bakers stress the significance of using proper measuring tools, such as dry measuring cups and spoons for dry ingredients and liquid measuring cups for wet ones. Flour, sugar, and other dry components should be leveled off for accuracy, while liquids should be measured at eye level for precise results. This attention to detail ensures that the chemistry of the recipe unfolds as intended, resulting in treats with the perfect texture and flavor.

Flour, a staple in many holiday recipes, is central to achieving the desired consistency and structure. Experts advise against scooping flour directly from the bag, as this can lead to compacted measurements. Instead, the recommended approach is to spoon the flour into the measuring cup and level it off with a straight edge. Additionally, using a kitchen scale can provide even greater accuracy when measuring flour for delicate baked goods like cookies or cakes. The objective is to strike a balance between too much and too little flour, as deviations can significantly impact the final outcome.

Beyond accurate measurements, the quality of ingredients is a cornerstone of successful holiday baking. Experts unanimously advocate for using fresh, high-quality ingredients to elevate the flavor profile of treats. The choice of butter, for instance, can be a game-changer in recipes where its rich flavor shines. Opting for unsalted butter allows for better control of the overall salt content while choosing European-style butter with higher fat content imparts a luxurious texture and taste. Similarly, the quality of vanilla extract, chocolate, and spices can markedly influence the depth and complexity of flavors in holiday treats.

Temperature plays a pivotal role in the alchemy of baking, and experts stress the importance of bringing ingredients to room temperature before incorporating them into recipes. Eggs, butter, and dairy products, when allowed to warm up, blend more seamlessly, resulting in better emulsification and a smoother batter. Cold ingredients can compromise the texture of baked goods, leading to uneven mixing and potential structural issues. Taking the time to plan and bring ingredients to room temperature enhances the baking process and contributes to the overall success of holiday treats.

The judicious use of leavening agents is a nuanced aspect of baking that experts navigate with precision. Baking powder and baking soda, while seemingly mundane, can profoundly impact the texture and rise of treats. Too much or too little of these leavening agents can result in dense or overly airy creations. Experts advise carefully measuring and sifting leavening agents with dry ingredients to ensure even distribution. Understanding the acidic or alkaline nature of other ingredients in the recipe allows bakers to adjust the leavening agents accordingly, achieving the perfect balance for light and fluffy holiday treats.

For those venturing into the realm of yeast-based treats, such as cinnamon rolls or stollen, understanding yeast behavior is paramount. Experts emphasize the vitality of fresh yeast, ensuring that it is within its expiration date for optimal performance. Activating yeast in warm (but not hot) liquid, often with a pinch of sugar, jumpstarts the fermentation process. Patience during the rising stages is crucial, and experts recommend placing the dough in a draft-free area covered with a damp cloth. This meticulous approach ensures that yeast-based holiday treats rise to their full potential, resulting in a delightful combination of flavor and texture.

Texture, a hallmark of exceptional baked goods, is a nuanced interplay of ingredients, techniques, and timing. Experts advise bakers to understand the role of fats in creating tender and moist treats. Choosing the right fat, whether butter, oil, or a combination of both, contributes to the desired texture. Creaming fats with sugar until light and fluffy, a technique often stressed by experts, incorporates air into the mixture, promoting a delicate crumb in cakes and cookies. Additionally, the careful folding of ingredients in light batters, such as those for soufflés or macarons, ensures a uniform texture without sacrificing aeration.

The mastery of flavor extends beyond ingredient selection to the art of balancing sweet and savory elements. Experts recommend an intentional approach to sweetness, advocating for the use of less sugar than some recipes might suggest. By slightly reducing sugar content, the nuanced flavors of other ingredients can shine, creating a more sophisticated and well-balanced taste profile. Similarly, the strategic use of salt heightens flavors, cutting through sweetness and enhancing the overall sensory experience. Experts often experiment with different types of salt, such as sea salt or fleur de sel, to add complexity to their creations.

While traditional recipes offer a solid foundation, experts encourage bakers to embrace creativity and personalize their holiday treats. Experimenting with flavor variations, adding unique twists to classic recipes, or infusing cultural influences can elevate the experience for both the baker and the consumer. Innovation, within the bounds of tried-and-true techniques, allows for the creation of signature holiday treats that reflect individual tastes and preferences. Experts celebrate the diversity of culinary traditions and encourage bakers to infuse their creations with a personal touch.

In the realm of pastry, the delicate dance of creating flaky and buttery crusts is a skill that experts have honed to perfection. Whether crafting pie crusts for holiday pies or laminating dough for croissants, the key lies in maintaining a cold environment. Cold butter, chilled water, and an excellent working surface are essential components of achieving the desired texture. Using a light touch, avoiding overworking the dough, is another fundamental principle stressed by experts. These meticulous steps contribute to the creation of pastry that is not only visually appealing but also irresistibly tender and flavorful.

Decorating holiday treats transforms them into edible works of art, and experts offer insights into achieving visually stunning results. For those working with royal icing, consistency is crucial for both outlining and flooding cookies. Experts recommend experimenting with the ratio of water to powdered sugar to achieve the desired thickness, ensuring that the icing sets evenly. Piping bags and tips, wielded with precision, allow for intricate designs and details. When working with fondant, experts advise rolling it out on a surface dusted with powdered sugar to prevent sticking and tearing. The artistry of decoration, while requiring practice, adds a festive and personalized touch to holiday treats.

Timing, the unsung hero of successful baking, is a facet that experts approach with meticulous attention. Understanding the nuances of individual ovens, recognizing signs of doneness, and respecting specified baking times are crucial to achieving perfect holiday treats. Experts often stress using visual and sensory cues, such as the golden-brown color of crusts or the springiness of a cake, to determine readiness. Oven thermometers, placed inside the oven, provide an accurate temperature gauge, allowing bakers to compensate for any variations and achieve consistent results.

The final touch to holiday treats often involves a sprinkle

of confectioners' sugar, a glaze drizzle, or a cocoa powder dusting. According to experts, presentation is not merely an aesthetic consideration but an integral part of the overall sensory experience. The artful arrangement of treats on a platter, the thoughtful use of garnishes, and the incorporation of seasonal elements contribute to the visual appeal. Experts often draw inspiration from nature, incorporating edible flowers, herbs, or fruits to enhance the festive ambiance. The marriage of flavor and presentation transforms holiday treats into a multisensory delight.

In conclusion, the creation of perfect holiday treats is an

art that combines science, skill, and a touch of magic. Drawing from the wisdom of culinary experts, bakers can navigate the intricacies of ingredient selection, technique, and timing to ensure that their creations taste exceptional and bring joy to those who indulge in them. The journey of baking, guided by expert tips, becomes a joyful exploration of flavors, textures, and creativity. As ovens warm and kitchens come alive with the aromas of holiday spices, these expert insights serve as companions on the path to crafting treats that embody the spirit of the season – a perfect blend of tradition, innovation, and the simple pleasure of sharing something sweet with those we hold dear.

CHAPTER XII

Beyond Baking: Crafting a Complete Christmas Experience

Pairing Treats with Festive Drinks

The holiday season is a time of indulgence, a time when kitchens come alive with the tantalizing aromas of freshly baked treats and cups brim with festive drinks that warm the soul. Beyond the intrinsic joy of baking and sipping, there lies a delightful art – the art of pairing treats with festive beverages. This culinary symphony, where flavors harmonize and enhance one another, transforms ordinary moments into memorable experiences. In this section, we explore the nuanced world of pairing holiday treats with the perfect beverages, unlocking the secrets behind combinations that evoke the season's spirit.

A classic starting point for pairing treats with festive

drinks lies in the heartwarming embrace of hot cocoa. The velvety richness of cocoa, with its deep chocolate notes, forms an ideal companion for many holiday treats. Picture a cozy evening adorned with the crackling sounds of a fireplace, the scent of evergreen in the air, and a cup of steaming hot cocoa cradled in your hands. Pairing this comforting beverage with a slice of chocolate cake adorned with a dusting of powdered sugar or a dollop of whipped cream creates a symphony of chocolate that is indulgent and satisfying. The dense, moist crumb of the cake complements the smoothness of the cocoa, resulting in a harmonious duet that is a testament to the enduring allure of chocolate during the holidays.

For those seeking a slightly more sophisticated pairing,

the marriage of spiced tea with gingerbread treats offers a delightful alternative. The robust, warming notes of chai or spiced black tea complement the intricate blend of spices in gingerbread cookies or cake. Imagine the subtle kick of cinnamon, ginger, and cloves mingling with the fragrant steam rising from a cup of spiced tea. The slightly sweet, molasses-infused goodness of gingerbread finds its ideal match in the aromatic complexity of the spiced tea. Together, they create a sensory experience that transcends the sum of its parts, inviting individuals to savor the warmth and nostalgia of the season.

As the winter chill settles in, the effervescent dance of sparkling cider takes center stage, offering a refreshing contrast to the sweetness of holiday treats. Apple-based treats, such as pies, tarts, or cinnamon-infused pastries, find a natural partner in the crisp effervescence of sparkling cider. The natural acidity and fruity undertones of the cider cleanse the palate between bites of rich, buttery pastry or flaky crust. The effervescence enhances the dining experience, cutting through the richness and leaving a tantalizing trail of fresh apple. This pairing captures the essence of a winter orchard, where the marriage of apples and bubbles creates a symphony of flavors that dance on the taste buds.

For those embracing the classic elegance of holiday desserts like pumpkin pie or pecan tarts, a velvety cup of eggnog is the ideal companion. The luscious, creamy texture of eggnog, with its notes of nutmeg and vanilla, harmonizes with the warm spices and silky fillings of these quintessential holiday treats. The eggnog's richness complements the pies' decadence, creating a luxurious combination that encapsulates the essence of holiday indulgence. The nutmeg in the eggnog bridges the flavors seamlessly, making each bite of pie a culinary celebration that resonates with the warmth and comfort of the season.

For those seeking a departure from traditional warm beverages, the sophisticated allure of a holiday cocktail can elevate the pairing experience. Picture a cranberry-infused martini served alongside delicate cranberry-orange shortbread cookies. The tartness of the cranberries in both the drink and the cookies creates a delightful interplay of flavors, with each sip and bite echoing the essence of the winter berry. The zesty orange notes in the cookies add a citrusy brightness that enhances the overall balance of the pairing. This combination exemplifies the art of pairing treats with festive drinks, where the complexity of a well-crafted cocktail amplifies the enjoyment of artisanal baked goods.

In the realm of savory treats, such as cheese platters adorned with holiday accouterments, pairing extends beyond baked goods to include a carefully selected assortment of wines. A robust red wine, like a Cabernet Sauvignon or Merlot, can complement the richness of aged cheeses and the sweetness of fig or apricot compotes. The tannins in the wine cut through the creaminess of the cheeses, while the fruity undertones harmonize with the sweet and savory elements on the platter. This sophisticated pairing transforms a cheese board into a culinary journey, where each sip and nibble unfolds a tapestry of flavors that dance on the palate.

The alchemy of pairing treats with festive drinks extends to coffee, a ubiquitous companion during the holiday season. Picture a steaming mug of spiced coffee, infused with cinnamon and nutmeg, served alongside a slice of moist, citrus-infused pound cake. The aromatic spices in the coffee enhance the zesty notes in the cake, creating a dynamic interplay of flavors. The robust character of the coffee grounds the sweetness of the cake, making each sip and bite a nuanced experience. This pairing captures the essence of a winter morning, where the comforting aroma of coffee mingles with the promise of a new day.

For those reveling in the nostalgia of childhood favorites, a pairing of hot apple cider and warm apple pie conjures images of idyllic family gatherings. The sweet, spiced warmth of the cider complements the flaky crust and tender apples in the pie. The contrast in temperatures, with the cider steaming and the pie at room temperature, adds a delightful sensory dimension to the pairing. This classic combination transports individuals to a cozy kitchen, where the aroma of baked apples and cinnamon permeates the air, and the clink of mugs and plates heralds the joyous sharing of holiday treats.

The interplay of textures and flavors is a hallmark of expertly paired treats and drinks, exemplified by the combination of creamy hot chocolate and crisp biscotti. The rich, velvety cocoa serves as a decadent dipping pool for the biscotti, which boasts a satisfying crunch. The juxtaposition of textures – the smooth, liquid cocoa against the toothsome biscotti – creates a delightful contrast that engages the senses. The biscotti, often studded with nuts or dried fruit, adds a layer of complexity to the pairing, making it a luxurious yet accessible indulgence that beckons individuals to savor the moment.

For those seeking a departure from the conventional, the fusion of treats and drinks opens up a world of creative possibilities. Consider pairing chai-spiced cupcakes with a chai-infused cocktail, creating a cohesive flavor experience that transcends traditional boundaries. The warm spices in the cupcakes echo the aromatic notes in the cocktail, resulting in a unexpected and delightful pairing. This avant-garde approach to pairing treats with drinks allows for exploration and innovation, inviting individuals to break free from tradition and create unique combinations that reflect their culinary sensibilities.

The art of pairing treats with festive drinks is not merely about matching flavors; it is an expression of creativity, a celebration of tradition, and a nod to the sensory delights that define the holiday season. Whether it's the comforting union of hot cocoa and chocolate cake, the refreshing dance of sparkling cider with apple pastries, or the nuanced interplay of spiced tea with gingerbread treats, each pairing tells a story. It narrates the essence of the season, capturing the warmth, nostalgia, and joy emanating from sharing treats and drinks with loved ones. As kitchens buzz with activity and cups overflow with holiday cheer, the art of pairing becomes a culinary journey, inviting individuals to savor the magic that unfolds when treats and drinks come together in perfect harmony.

Incorporating Baked Goods into Holiday Celebrations

Holiday celebrations worldwide are often marked by a plethora of traditions, each unique to its cultural context. Among the myriad customs that define these festive occasions, incorporating baked goods stands out as a universal and cherished practice. From elaborate gingerbread houses to the humblest sugar cookies, the art of baking transcends borders, bringing families and communities together in the spirit of joy and shared indulgence. This section explores the profound significance of incorporating baked goods into holiday celebrations, delving into the historical roots of this tradition, the diverse array of festive treats, and the communal bonds forged through baking.

To comprehend the deep-seated connection between baked goods and holidays, one must delve into the historical tapestry of human traditions. Baking, in various forms, has been an integral part of cultural celebrations for centuries. Ancient civilizations, such as the Egyptians and Greeks, used bread as a sacred offering during religious ceremonies, establishing a precedent for the spiritual connection between baked goods and communal festivities. As civilizations evolved, so too did the art of baking, with each culture contributing its unique flavors and techniques to the global tapestry of culinary traditions. In medieval Europe, the Yule log cake became a symbol of the winter solstice, while in the Middle East, the fragrant scent of baklava wafted through the air during Eid celebrations. The threads of these historical practices continue to weave through contemporary holiday baking, connecting us to our ancestors and the rich tapestry of human experience.

The spectrum of baked goods associated with holidays is as diverse as the cultures that produce them. Christmas, for instance, is synonymous with a delightful array of festive treats. The ubiquitous gingerbread cookies, adorned with intricate icing designs, evoke a sense of nostalgia and whimsy. Stollen, a traditional German fruitcake, graces tables during the holiday season, its dense, sweet interior enveloped powdered sugar. Meanwhile, the smell of cinnamon and nutmeg wafts from kitchens as families prepare pumpkin pies for Thanksgiving in the United States. Similarly, Diwali, the Hindu festival of lights, sees the creation of an assortment of sweets like gulab jamun and jalebi, symbolizing the triumph of light over darkness. The universality of incorporating baked goods into holiday celebrations underscores the power of food to transcend cultural boundaries and evoke a shared sense of joy.

Beyond the delectable flavors and fragrances, baking becomes a communal experience that fosters connection and strengthens bonds. Families and friends gather in kitchens, measuring ingredients, sharing stories, and passing down recipes through generations. The tactile nature of baking, from kneading dough to decorating cookies, engages multiple senses and creates a sensory experience that is as emotionally fulfilling as it is gastronomically satisfying. The shared effort of preparing a holiday feast fosters a sense of unity and belonging, reinforcing the social fabric that binds individuals together. Moreover, the exchange of recipes becomes a form of cultural transmission, ensuring that traditional baked goods remain honored in holiday celebrations.

Incorporating baked goods into holiday celebrations also serves as a powerful form of self-expression. Bakers often invest time and creativity in crafting visually stunning and delicious treats that reflect their style and cultural identity. Presenting a lovingly baked cake or a batch of cookies becomes a gesture of generosity and goodwill, symbolizing the spirit of giving that defines many holiday traditions. In this way, baked goods become a form of edible art, with each creation telling a story and conveying a message of celebration, gratitude, or love. The sense of accomplishment derived from creating something beautiful and delicious enhances the joy of sharing these treats with others.

Furthermore, baking and sharing holiday treats extends beyond the confines of individual households to encompass the broader community. Potluck gatherings, cookie exchanges, and bake sales are common occurrences during the holiday season, providing opportunities for individuals to share their culinary creations with a wider audience. These communal events showcase the diverse array of baked goods that characterize different cultural traditions and create a sense of camaraderie among neighbors, colleagues, and community members. The simple act of offering someone a homemade treat becomes a gesture of goodwill, fostering connections and spreading the joy of the season.

While the incorporation of baked goods into holiday celebrations undoubtedly brings people together, it is essential to recognize the challenges and considerations that accompany this tradition. In an era marked by increasing awareness of dietary restrictions and health concerns, the inclusivity of holiday treats becomes pertinent. The prevalence of allergies, dietary restrictions, and lifestyle choices necessitates a thoughtful approach to baking that accommodates diverse needs. Fortunately, the growing popularity of alternative ingredients and creative adaptations allows individuals to enjoy the tradition of holiday baking while respecting various dietary preferences and restrictions.

In conclusion, incorporating baked goods into holiday celebrations serves as a timeless and universal tradition that bridges the past and present connects diverse cultures, and strengthens communal bonds. From the historical roots of baking as a sacred offering to the diverse array of treats associated with different celebrations, the tradition of holiday baking embodies the essence of shared joy and cultural expression. The act of baking itself becomes a communal experience, fostering connection and unity among individuals and communities.

As we gather around festive tables laden with cookies, cakes, and pies, we partake in a global celebration that transcends borders, creating a tapestry of flavors and traditions that enrich the human experience.

CHAPTER XIII

Global Christmas Baking Traditions

Exploring Unique Holiday Treats from Around the World

Holiday celebrations manifest in a kaleidoscope of traditions, customs, and, perhaps most delightfully, culinary creations. The world over, communities unite in the spirit of festivity, expressing their unique cultural identities through the art of food. Beyond the familiar trappings of tinsel and twinkling lights, the diverse array of holiday treats serves as a window into the rich tapestry of global traditions. This section embarks on a delectable journey to explore unique holiday treats from around the world, delving into the historical and cultural contexts that give rise to these distinctive culinary delights.

In Italy, the celebration of Christmas is complete with the presence of Panettone, a sweet bread studded with candied fruits and raisins. With its origins rooted in Milan, this tall, domed confection has become synonymous with Italian holiday festivities. Legend has it that Panettone was created by a young nobleman to win the heart of his beloved, a commoner named Toni. The bread, leavened to a light and airy texture, embodies the essence of the season. Shared among family and friends, Panettone is often presented as a token of goodwill, encapsulating the warmth and generosity of Italian holiday traditions.

Traveling to the southern hemisphere, Christmas in Australia takes on a unique flavor with the introduction of the Pavlova. This meringue-based dessert, named after the Russian ballerina Anna Pavlova, is a crisp meringue shell delicately cradling a soft and marshmallowy interior. Crowned with a luscious layer of whipped cream and an assortment of fresh fruits, the Pavlova embodies the sun-kissed, laid-back holiday spirit of the Australian summer. The debate over the dessert's origin—Australia or New Zealand—adds a playful rivalry to the enjoyment of this light and refreshing treat.

In the heart of Mexico, the Christmas season is heralded by the arrival of Tamales. These savory or sweet-filled masa pockets, wrapped in corn husks, trace their roots back to ancient Aztec and Maya traditions. Tamales are a labor of love, often prepared in large quantities and shared among extended family and neighbors. The communal aspect of tamale-making fosters a sense of unity and togetherness, aligning with the spirit of the holiday season. From the spicy and savory to the sweet and fruity, tamale fillings' diversity reflects Mexican cuisine's rich cultural tapestry.

Crossing the Atlantic to the Nordic region, Sweden introduces the tradition of Pepparkakor during the Christmas season. These spiced gingerbread cookies, intricately shaped into various forms, have become a staple of Swedish holiday celebrations. The warm blend of cinnamon, ginger, and cloves infuses the air as families gather to bake and decorate Pepparkakor. The cookies are not merely a treat for the taste buds; they also serve as ornaments adorning Christmas trees. Hanging these edible decorations transforms the Christmas tree into a fragrant and festive display, creating a multisensory experience for all who partake in the holiday festivities.

In Japan, celebrating the New Year brings forth the tradition of Osechi Ryori, a meticulously crafted assortment of dishes symbolizing prosperity, longevity, and good fortune. Among the array of delicacies, Mochi—a sticky rice cake with a chewy consistency—holds a place of honor. Mochi-making is a communal event, with families and communities collating the glutinous rice into a sticky, elastic mass. The resulting mochi is then shaped into various forms, often filled with sweet red bean paste or savory ingredients. The act of sharing and consuming mochi during the New Year festivities is believed to bring good luck and unity to those who partake in this Japanese tradition.

Venturing into the Middle East, the celebration of Eid al-Fitr is accompanied by the preparation and sharing of Ma'amoul. These intricately molded, shortbread-like cookies are filled with dates, nuts, or figs and dusted with powdered sugar. Ma'amoul holds cultural significance, not only for its delicious taste but also for the artistry of crafting the wooden molds used to shape the cookies. Families often pass down these molds from generation to generation, creating a tangible link to the past. The sharing of Ma'amoul during Eid represents the joy of breaking the fast and the bonds of community that characterize this Islamic celebration.

In the Philippines, the approach of Christmas heralds the season of Bibingka. This rice cake, traditionally cooked over hot coals and topped with salted eggs and grated coconut, is a beloved holiday treat. Bibingka vendors shop near churches during the nine-day Simbang Gabi, a series of pre-dawn Masses leading up to Christmas. The warm and comforting aroma of Bibingka wafting through the air becomes synonymous with the anticipation of Christmas in the Philippines, creating a sensory connection to the festive season.

Transitioning to the African continent, specifically Ethiopia, the celebration of Timket, or Epiphany, is marked by the preparation of Dulet. This spicy and hearty dish consists of minced meat, liver, and tripe, cooked with spices and herbs. Dulet is often enjoyed during communal gatherings, adding a savory dimension to the festivities. The dish exemplifies the cultural significance of food as a means of bringing people together, fostering camaraderie, and reinforcing community bonds during religious celebrations.

The exploration of unique holiday treats from around the world reveals the diversity of flavors and ingredients and the cultural stories embedded in each culinary creation. These festive treats serve as edible expressions of heritage, history, and shared values, bridging the past and the present. As we savor these delectable delights, we indulge our taste buds and partake in a global celebration of diversity, unity, and the joyous spirit that unites us all during the holiday season.

Adapting International Flavors in Your Christmas Kitchen

As the holiday season unfolds, the kitchen becomes a hub of festive activity, with the aromas of spices, sweets, and savory delights filling the air. While traditional holiday recipes hold a special place in our hearts, there is an exciting culinary world to explore by incorporating international flavors into the Christmas kitchen. This section embarks on a flavorful journey, exploring the rich tapestry of global cuisines and offering insights into how you can infuse your Christmas menu with international flair.

With its sun-kissed landscapes and robust culinary traditions, the Mediterranean region provides a treasure trove of flavors to elevate your Christmas feast. Consider starting with a Mezze platter featuring hummus, tzatziki, and muhammara, accompanied by warm pita bread. The herb-infused goodness of Greek Spanakopita, a spinach and feta-filled pastry, adds a savory touch. For the main course, embrace the aromatic allure of Moroccan cuisine with a tagine, slow-cooked to perfection with a blend of spices, dried fruits, and tender meats. Conclude the Mediterranean-inspired feast with the sweet indulgence of baklava, its layers of phyllo dough, nuts, and honey offering a delightful contrast of textures.

Asia, with its diverse culinary traditions, offers a myriad of flavors that can bring a unique twist to your Christmas celebration. Start with an appetizer of Vietnamese spring rolls, their freshness and vibrant flavors setting the tone for the meal. For the main course, consider a fusion of East and West with a miso-glazed roast turkey or a fragrant Thai curry featuring seasonal vegetables and aromatic herbs. Accompany the main course with Japanese-inspired sesame soy Brussels sprouts for a contemporary twist. Conclude the feast with the delicate sweetness of mango sticky rice, a Thai dessert that adds a tropical touch to your Christmas table.

With its bold and vibrant flavors, Latin American cuisine offers a festive feast that can infuse your Christmas celebration with a lively spirit. Start with classic guacamole paired with crisp tortilla chips, setting the stage for a flavorful journey. Dive into the heartiness of a Mexican mole poblano, a rich and complex sauce featuring chocolate, chili peppers, and spices, elevating your Christmas turkey or roast. Add a side of Peruvian quinoa salad for a nutritious and colorful complement. Conclude the Latin American fiesta with the indulgence of churros served with a decadent chocolate dipping sauce, bringing a sweet finale to your international Christmas menu.

With its diverse culinary traditions, Europe offers a sophisticated touch to your Christmas table. Begin with the elegance of French onion soup, its rich broth and gooey Gruyère cheese setting the stage for a refined meal. Embrace the Italian tradition of the Feast of the Seven Fishes with a seafood pasta featuring an array of delicacies from the sea. Complement the main course with the hearty flavors of German potato dumplings or French gratin dauphinois. Conclude the European-inspired feast with a classic English trifle, layering sponge cake, custard, and berries for a sweet and indulgent conclusion to your Christmas celebration.

Africa's diverse and vibrant cuisines offer a wealth of spices and flavors that can add a bold and exciting dimension to your Christmas menu. Start with an appetizer of South African bunny chow, a flavorful curry served in a hollowed-out loaf of bread, setting the tone for a festive meal. Explore the savory delights of Moroccan bastilla, a flaky pastry filled with spiced meat and nuts, adding a touch of North African elegance to your table. Accompany the main course with a side of jollof rice, a West African dish known for its aromatic blend of spices and tomato-infused rice. Conclude the feast with the sweet warmth of South African malva pudding, a sticky caramel dessert that adds a comforting touch to your Christmas celebration.

Adapting international flavors into your Christmas kitchen requires a thoughtful approach to ensure a harmonious fusion of tastes and textures. Start by exploring the individual elements of each cuisine, understanding the key ingredients and flavor profiles. Experiment with small batches to fine-tune the balance of flavors and textures before incorporating a new dish into your holiday menu. Consider the cultural context of each dish, appreciating the traditions and stories behind the flavors you are introducing. Be open to creative reinterpretations, allowing the essence of a dish to inspire rather than strictly adhering to traditional recipes.

In conclusion, infusing your Christmas kitchen with international flavors offers a culinary adventure that transcends borders and traditions. Whether you explore the Mediterranean, Asia, Latin America, Europe, or Africa, the key lies in embracing the diversity of global cuisines and bringing a sense of curiosity to your holiday cooking. As you embark on this flavorful journey, you create a memorable Christmas feast and celebrate the richness of human culinary creativity, connecting with cultures from around the world through the universal language of food.

CHAPTER XIV

Reflections and New Traditions

Cherishing Memories of Christmas Baking

The air is infused with warm and familiar vanilla, cinnamon, and nutmeg scents. The kitchen is a bustling hub of activity, filled with laughter, the clinking of measuring spoons, and the rhythmic hum of an electric mixer. Christmas baking, a cherished tradition in countless households, is not just about creating delectable treats but is woven into the fabric of cherished memories and heartwarming moments. This section delves into the intimate connection between Christmas and baking, exploring the sensory delights, the familial bonds forged, and the enduring legacy of recipes passed down through generations.

At the heart of Christmas baking lies a sensory journey that transcends the simple act of creating confections. The scent of cookies baking in the oven evokes a sense of nostalgia, transporting individuals to the cozy kitchens of their childhoods. The earthy aroma of gingerbread, shortbread's buttery richness, and sugar cookies' sweet perfume are more than just olfactory experiences; they are threads that weave through the tapestry of cherished memories. Each whiff of vanilla extract or freshly ground spices becomes a time capsule, unlocking moments of joy, anticipation, and the unmistakable spirit of the holiday season.

Beyond the sensory pleasures, Christmas baking serves as a vehicle for the creation of lasting memories and the strengthening of familial bonds. Families come together in the kitchen, donning aprons and dusting countertops with flour, to embark on the annual tradition of crafting holiday treats. The laughter of children, the teasing banter between siblings, and the shared sense of purpose create an atmosphere of joy and togetherness. Grandmothers pass down time-honored recipes to wide- eyed grandchildren, imparting not just the ingredients and techniques but the stories and traditions that accompany each dish. In these moments, the kitchen transforms into a crucible of love, where baking becomes a language that speaks of connection and continuity.

The recipes themselves, often guarded like treasured family heirlooms, carry a profound significance in Christmas baking. These recipes are not merely lists of ingredients and instructions but are imbued with the personal touches, variations, and anecdotes that give them life. The stained and tattered recipe cards, lovingly scribbled notes in the margins, and handwritten instructions passed down through generations become a tangible link to the past. Baking from a family recipe is a way of honoring those who came before, a gesture that transcends time and connects individuals to the roots of their familial heritage. In this sense, the kitchen becomes a sacred space where tradition and innovation merge, creating a culinary legacy that extends far beyond the holiday season.

Christmas baking is a journey of creativity and self-expression, allowing individuals to infuse their personality into the treats they create. Whether it's the meticulous decoration of sugar cookies, the inventive use of seasonal ingredients, or the playful experimentation with traditional recipes, baking becomes a canvas for self-expression. The act of creating something with one's hands fosters a sense of accomplishment and pride, turning the kitchen into a space where individuals can channel their creativity and make a unique mark on the holiday festivities. In this way, Christmas baking becomes not only a means of nourishing the body but a form of edible art, with each creation serving as a reflection of the baker's personality and the spirit of the season.

As the cookies cool on the racks and the aroma of freshly baked goods permeates the air, the act of sharing becomes a central theme of Christmas baking. Plates of cookies are exchanged with neighbors, colleagues, and friends, becoming edible tokens of goodwill and camaraderie. Giving and receiving homemade treats creates a sense of community and shared joy, transcending cultural and religious boundaries. In a world often characterized by hustle and bustle, the simple act of gifting a batch of cookies becomes a powerful gesture of warmth and connection, echoing the season's true spirit.

In the contemporary era, where the pace of life is often frenetic, Christmas baking provides a respite—a moment to slow down and savor the simple pleasures. The act of measuring ingredients, the rhythmic stirring of batter, and the patient waiting for cookies to rise in the oven become a form of mindfulness, grounding individuals in the present moment. Baking becomes a therapeutic endeavor, offering solace and a welcome respite from the stresses of daily life. The tactile nature of the process, from kneading dough to shaping cookies, engages the senses and creates a sensory experience that is as emotionally fulfilling as it is gastronomically satisfying.

However, the tradition of Christmas baking is not static; it evolves with the times, reflecting changing tastes, dietary preferences, and cultural influences. Individuals now seek innovative recipes that cater to a spectrum of nutritional needs, incorporating gluten-free, vegan, or allergy-friendly alternatives. The traditional gingerbread may find itself sharing the spotlight with matcha-flavored cookies or tahini-infused treats. The fusion of international flavors, once considered avant-garde, now adds a contemporary twist to classic recipes, expanding the culinary horizons of Christmas baking and catering to the diverse palates of a globalized world.

In conclusion, Christmas baking is more than a culinary tradition; it is a holistic experience that engages the senses, nurtures familial bonds, and creates lasting memories. The scents, tastes, and textures of holiday treats are intertwined with the fabric of cherished moments, becoming a bridge between generations and a repository of family stories. As the aroma of Christmas cookies wafts through the air and the kitchen becomes a hub of activity, individuals partake in a timeless celebration that transcends the act of baking itself. In the kitchen's warmth, amid flour-dusted countertops and the laughter of loved ones, the true essence of Christmas baking is revealed—a celebration of love, connection, and the enduring magic of the holiday season.

Starting Your Own Family Baking Traditions

In the hustle and bustle of modern life, where time seems to slip through our fingers like sand, starting and maintaining family traditions has taken on newfound significance. Among these, the practice of creating and perpetuating family baking traditions stands out as a delightful and rewarding endeavor. Beyond the delectable aromas and flavors that waft through the kitchen, baking together fosters bonds, creates lasting memories, and imparts a sense of continuity that transcends generations. This section explores the importance of starting your family baking traditions, delving into the psychological, cultural, and social dimensions that make this practice a recipe for shared memories and meaningful connections.

Baking is not just a culinary activity; it's a therapeutic and communal experience. The act of measuring, mixing, and creating together in the kitchen can be a powerful stress reliever, offering a unique form of family therapy. The tactile nature of baking engages all the senses, providing a break from the digital world and allowing family members to connect on a more personal level. As the scent of fresh cookies or bread fills the air, the kitchen becomes a haven for emotional expression, fostering open communication and strengthening familial bonds.

Baking traditions often carry with them a rich tapestry of cultural heritage.Passed down through generations, recipes become vessels for preserving and transmitting cultural identity. Whether it's a cherished recipe for Grandma's apple pie or a unique twist on a traditional holiday dessert, baking becomes a tangible link to the past. The process of teaching and learning these recipes not only imparts culinary skills but also serves as a means of preserving cultural rituals, values, and stories, ensuring they are not lost in the currents of time.

The aroma of baking cookies, the laughter shared while frosting a cake, and the anticipation of waiting for the timer to ding — these moments form the tapestry of family memories. Baking provides a canvas upon which families can paint their unique stories. From celebrating birthdays with homemade cakes to the annual tradition of baking holiday cookies, these rituals create a repository of shared experiences that family members can revisit and reminisce about throughout their lives. In this way, baking traditions contribute to the construction of a family's collective memory.

Baking is an art as much as it is a science, allowing for creativity and innovation in the kitchen. Encouraging family members, especially children, to experiment with flavors, textures, and presentations fosters a sense of creativity and curiosity. This freedom to explore within the confines of a recipe nurtures not only culinary skills but also a broader mindset of creative problem-solving and thinking outside the box — skills that extend beyond the kitchen into various aspects of life.

In today's fast-paced world, finding quality time to spend with family can be a challenge. Family baking traditions offer a remedy to this modern dilemma. Whether it's a weekend baking session or a monthly family bake-off, these traditions carve out dedicated time for families to come together. This intentional time spent in the kitchen is an investment in relationships, creating a sanctuary where the distractions of the outside world can be set aside, and genuine connections can be nurtured

Baking is an excellent medium for imparting essential life skills. From honing mathematical abilities through precise measurements to cultivating patience while waiting for dough to rise, the kitchen becomes a classroom for practical life lessons. Moreover, the delegation of tasks during baking sessions instills a sense of responsibility and teamwork, teaching family members the importance of collaboration and shared effort.

Family baking traditions are not static; they evolve with time and circumstances. While the core recipes may remain the same, families often adapt traditions to accommodate changing tastes, dietary preferences, and lifestyles. This adaptability allows traditions to endure, ensuring that they remain relevant and inclusive across generations. The ability to adapt baking traditions reflects the resilience and flexibility inherent in strong family units.

In the intricate tapestry of family life, baking traditions weave threads of connection, warmth, and love. Beyond the simple act of mixing flour, sugar, and eggs, family baking traditions offer a platform for the creation of enduring memories, the transmission of cultural heritage, and the nurturing of essential life skills. As families gather in the kitchen, armed with aprons and recipes passed down through the ages, they not only produce delicious treats but also craft a legacy of togetherness. Starting your own family baking traditions is not just about what ends up on the dessert table; it's about savoring the journey, one shared moment at a time. In the comforting embrace of flour-dusted hands and sugary smiles, families find a sanctuary where the past, present, and future blend seamlessly, creating a recipe for a life well-li

CONCLUSION

In the enchanting pages of "Unveiling the Magic of Christmas Baking: A Whisk of Holiday Magic," readers are transported into a world where the spirit of Christmas is intricately woven into the art of baking. As the final chapter of this culinary journey unfolds, it becomes evident that this e-book is not just a compilation of recipes but a heartfelt ode to the magic that grows in the kitchen during the holiday season.

The e-book, with its enticing title, serves as a key to

unlocking the wonders of Christmas baking. More than a mere introduction, it is a guide to infuse the festive season with a sprinkle of joy, a dash of tradition, and a generous dollop of shared experiences. Through its virtual pages, the authors beckon readers to embark on a culinary adventure beyond ingredients and instructions, inviting them to embrace the true essence of Christmas— the spirit of togetherness.

One of the remarkable aspects of "A Whisk of Holiday Magic" is its ability to seamlessly bridge the gap between tradition and innovation. The e-book expertly navigates the delicate balance between timeless classics and contemporary twists, offering recipes catering to the nostalgia of cherished family traditions and the excitement of creating something new. This duality is a testament to the versatility of Christmas baking, where the familiar and the novel coexist harmoniously.

Throughout the e-book, the authors share recipes and impart a sense of the cultural and emotional significance of each dish. The stories behind the recipes, anecdotes of holiday gatherings, and personal reflections infuse the content with a warmth that transcends the digital medium. As readers flip through the pages, they are not just following instructions but partaking in a narrative that celebrates the richness of holiday traditions.

The e-book stands as a testament to the belief that Christmas baking is not merely a culinary activity but a means of creating lasting memories. Each recipe becomes a vessel for storytelling, a way to pass down family lore, and a medium through which generations connect. The act of baking, as portrayed in the e-book, transforms the kitchen into a festive haven where laughter, love, and the aroma of freshly baked goodies blend into a symphony of holiday joy.

As readers conclude "Unveiling the Magic of Christmas Baking," they find themselves equipped with a collection of delectable recipes and a newfound inspiration to elevate their holiday celebrations. The e-book, with its charming narratives and mouthwatering visuals, leaves a lasting impression, encouraging readers not merely to replicate recipes but to infuse their magic into the kitchen.

Essentially, "A Whisk of Holiday Magic" is a gift to everyone seeking to make Christmas baking a meaningful and memorable tradition. It is a reminder that, beyond the ingredients and the finished products, the true magic lies in the moments created, the stories shared, and the love baked into every dish. As the digital pages close, readers are left with more than just a guidebook—they carry the keys to a world where the magic of Christmas and the joy of baking converge into a harmonious celebration of life, love, and the festive spirit.

Thank you for buying and reading/ listening to our book. If you found this book useful/ helpful please take a few minutes and leave a review on the platform where you purchased our book. Your feedback matters greatly to us.

9 798869 125163